AYSHFORD'S

Court, Chapel and Community

by

Charles Scott-Fox

Published for Friends of Friendless Churches

Published by
Charles Scott-Fox
for Friends of Friendless Churches

Copyright © Charles Scott-Fox

ISBN: 978-0-9547013-4-5

Also by Charles Scott-Fox
Cyril Fox – Archaeologist Extraordinary
Devon County Prison, Exeter
Bickham House and the Short(e) Family
Sampford Peverell – The Village, Church,
Chapel and Rectories (Ed)

Printed by
Peninsular Services (UK) Limited

CONTENTS

Friends of Friendless Churcles	iv
Information for Visitors	iv
Acknowledgements	v
List of Illustrations	vi
Ayshford Court and Chapel from Ayshford Bridge	viii
Preface *by Matthew Saunders MBE, Hon. Director Friends of Friendless Churches*	ix
Extract from Benjamin Donn's map of Devonshire 1765	x
The Ayshford Sanford Inheritance	1
Ayshford Court	17
Ayshford Chapel	31
The Ayshford Community	39
Bibliography	50
Appendix I – The Ayshford Inheritance and Family Tree	52
Appendix II - The Sanford Inheritance and Family Tree	54

Friends of Friendless Churches

The Friends of Friendless Churches was founded in 1957 by Ivor Bulmer Thomas, former MP and minister in Clement Atlee's government, writer, journalist and churchman. The Society now owns some 40 churches and chapels, saved from demolition and dereliction, half in England and half in Wales. This includes two properties in Devon, Ayshford Chapel and the mediaeval ruins at South Huish in the South Hams. Unlike the Churches Conservation Trust, of which Ivor Thomas was also the first chairman, the Friends can take private chapels like Ayshford and this is an area where we expect to have to expand our holding in future.

All of the Friends churches and chapels are listed and illustrated on the website. Many are available for visits during the day without having to secure a key and most of those that are locked are open for Heritage Open Days in September.

The Friends operate a joint membership scheme with the Ancient Monuments Society. Join one and you join the other without extra charge. Members receive three newsletters a year, an annual volume of Transactions, and information on relevant events and books. The Friends Annual General Meeting is nearly always held in one of its own churches and that of the Ancient Monuments Society in an historic building not normally open to the public.

Anyone seeking further information should contact the office of the Hon. Director, Matthew Saunders, at:

Friends of Friendless Churches, St.Ann's Vestry Hall,
2 Church Entry, London EC4V 5HB.
Tel: 020 7236 3934 email: office@friendsoffriendlesschurches.org.uk
Website: www. friendsoffriendlesschurches.org.uk
Registered Charity 1113097
Registered Company 119137

Information for Visitors

Ayshford Chapel is normally kept locked but is opened for visitors for four days at the beginning of September. At other times visitors may request the key to the South Door from Mrs Kelland at Ayshford Court Farm (opposite the field entrance to the chapel field) (Tel. 01884 820271). Please take care to close the gate behind you and do not take dogs as there are free range chickens and sheep in the field.

Ayshford Court is a private house and is not open to visitors.

Acknowledgements

Most of us, given the privilege of living in a town or village that clearly has ancient origins, will have an interest in its history. Moving into the hamlet of Ayshford in 1973, my interest was stimulated by Mrs Merrey, the then owner of Ayshford Court, who gave me copies of Ralegh Radford's notes and a letter from W.G. Copeland that summarised their views on the history of the Court and St. Michael's Chapel. Some thirty years later, I decided to try to expand on their findings, taking advantage of the excellent facilities offered by both the Devon and Somerset Record Offices. It was at the latter, that I had the good fortune to meet the genealogist Heather Ayshford. Her interest and contribution to this volume has been invaluable; without her generous gift of unlimited access to her Ayshford family researches, the tale of their inheritance would be sadly incomplete. On being informed of the project, William Ayshford Sanford, the current Lord of the Manor of Burlescombe (and Ayshford), suggested that I included photographs of his portraits of Henry and Amy Ayshford and Henry Sanford, and the Ayshford Coat of Arms. His incredible family archive, now in the possession of the Somerset Record Office, is the source of most of the rest of the information that relates to the Ayshford Sanford Inheritance. I met Matthew Saunders, Honorary Director of Friends of Friendless Churches, when his charity was overseeing the restoration of Ayshford chapel. As well as giving me his unqualified support for this book, he introduced me to Mrs Jeanne James, whose article on the chapel, published originally by Devon & Cornwall Notes and Queries, was an inspiration and a source of innumerable references. Her personal involvement, and that of her fellow historian Mrs Priscilla Flower-Smith, has been very much appreciated. I am most grateful to Richard and Lucy Acfield, the present owners of Ayshford Court, for allowing me free access to this lovely old building, and to Neil MacDonald for the majority of photographs used to illustrate my text. Additionally, my thanks are extended to Peter Bowers, chairman of the Sampford Peverell Society, and members for providing information on other relevant documents, including the Ayshford Sanford conveyance of 1811, preparation of the typescript and illustrations for publication, and, not least, for proof reading my un-edited script. Finally, publication of this volume has been greatly assisted by a generous donation from Williams De Broë.

CSF
October 2008

List of illustrations

Figure	Title	Page
Cover	Ayshford Court and Chapel from Ayshford Bridge	viii
Frontispiece	Extract from Benjamin Donn's map of Devonshire 1765 *(Devon Record Office)*	x
1	Ayshford Coat of Arms *(Ayshford Sanford collection)*	5
2	Nicholas Ayshford (1507-1585) tomb *(Burlescombe Parish Church)*	6
3	Roger Ayshford (1537-1611) wall monument *(Burlescombe Parish Church)*	6
4	Henry Ayshford (1576-1650) *(Ayshford Sanford collection)*	7
5	Amy Ayshford (née Bluett, m. Henry Ayshford 1599) d. 1659 *(Ayshford Sanford collection)*	7
6	Arthur Ayshford (1601-ca.1645) wall monument *(Burlescombe Parish Church)*	8
7	Henry Sanford (1612-1644) *(Ayshford Sanford collection)*	10
8	Nynehead Court (ca.1792) *(Nynehead & District Local History Society)*	11
9	Nynehead Court garden (ca. 1870) *(Nynehead & District Local History Society)*	12
10	Ayshford Chapel Bell-cote	13
11	Ayshford Court - the Hall	17
12	Ayshford Court ground and first floor plans	18
13	Ayshford Court west wing from the garden	19
14	Detail - jointed cruck	20
15	Ayshford Court west wing from the inner courtyard	20
16	Detail - two-light oak-pegged window (ca.1500)	20
17	Hall - ingle-nook fireplace	21
18	Ayshford Court - Victorian porch and corner extension	21
19	West wing - first floor passage	22
20	Ayshford Court - west wing 19th century extensions	22
21	Ayshford Court south wing from the canal	23
22	South wing - mullioned stone window	23
23	South wing - bedroom fireplace and moulded ceiling	24
24	South wing - Court Room fireplace and moulded ceiling	25
25	Detail - priest's hole in Court Room chimney	25
26	Extract from 1839 Tithe Commisioner's map of Devon *(Devon Record Office)*	26
27	Ayshford Court - Gatehouse	27
28	South-facing long barn	27
29	Ayshford Chapel from the south-west	30
30	15th century Chancel screen and wagon roof	32

31	South door	33
32	Henry Ayshford (1664-1666) tomb	34
33	John Ayshford (ca.1641-1690) wall monument	34
34	19th century perpendicular style windows	35
35	East end window - central inscription of Te Deum glazing sequence	36
36	Detail - Logo of stained glass artist John Toms of Wellington	36
37	West end window	36
38	Putlog hole	37
39	Chapel undergoing repairs 2002	38
40	Ayshford House, Lower Ayshford Farm and Ayshford Cottages	39
41	Ayshford 'Street' Population Graph 1066-2007	42
42	Ayshford Estate map ca. 1760 *(Devon Record Office)*	44
43	Ayshford House	45
44	Ayshford Cottages	46
45	Lower Ayshford Farm	47
46	Locks Cottage	48

In addition to the attributions given above, Friends of Friendless Churches wishes to add their appreciation to Apex Photo Agency, Christopher Dalton, Colin Findlay and Neil MacDonald for the use of their photographs for this book.

Ayshford Court and St Michael's Chapel from Ayshford Bridge *(Neil MacDonald)*

Preface

The small hamlet of Ayshford is to be found half way between the Mid-Devon villages of Sampford Peverell and Westleigh and sits on a seam of New Red Sandstone that is the dominant feature of the landscape to the west of the M5 Motorway. Today this hamlet consists of barely half a dozen properties, but it was a substantial manorial holding in Domesday with records going back to Saxon times. This history of the community, established by the Ayshford family, is intended to provide the visitor with an insight into its origins and the buildings that remain.

Although there is a minor road from Holbrook Junction on the Devon Link Road to Westleigh, Ayshford is best approached by walking from Sampford Peverell along the towpath of the Grand Western Canal for about a mile and a half. Passing under Ayshford Bridge two enormous ancient oaks on the western bank provide a picturesque frame for a 15th C chapel with the Tudor Ayshford Court and its small walled garden behind. At this point the canal is well banked up. To the east the visitor can look down some six or seven metres to the road and the roofs of the remaining buildings that were once part of a thriving community formerly known as Ayshford Street. Construction of the canal has dramatically altered the landscape for much of its length, especially where steep embankments have been required to maintain the contour line, and streams have been enclosed in culverts or occasionally built over as aqueducts. Prior to 1812, the land below Ayshford Court fell gradually towards the hamlet, with the millstream from an old water-powered grist mill situated just below the chapel. Today, most of the land between the canal and the Court can be seen to have been levelled, except for the deep hollow now occupied by the trunks of those two great oaks, which provides the only visual evidence of that ancient mill.

The Friends of Friendless Churches are the proud owners of an extended lease of the chapel and are delighted to have been able to publish this definitive account of its history and that of the village in general. Local history can be rocky in its scholarship, but the author here has combined authority with easy readability. It represents the summation of hours of research and is driven by a quiet determined affection for this corner of one of England's most beautiful counties. The book is also a symbol of the relationship between a national, albeit very small, organisation like ours, and local people without whom we cannot begin to safeguard the 40 churches and chapels in England and Wales for which we are responsible. All of the chapel's immediate neighbours help by keeping the building clean, opening it for Heritage Open Days and holding the key. We can save the churches from destruction, we can repair them, but we need local people to cherish them.

Charles Scott-Fox has now provided a model guide-book, for the chapel's steady stream of visitors and all those interested in Devon's history. I hope you enjoy this fascinating story of an ancient community and that it enriches your visit to the chapel.

Matthew Saunders MBE
Honorary Director, Friends of Friendless Churches
October 2008

Extract from Benjamin Donn's map of Devonshire 1765 (Devon Record Office)

THE AYSHFORD SANFORD INHERITANCE

Ayshford is of particular interest to historians as one of very few places in Devon listed in the pre-Conquest charter of 958 AD[1] with an estate, combined with Boehill, of 2.5 hides[2] (about 300 acres) of arable, pasture, woodland and waste. This estate, which had been granted to Eadheah by King Edwy of Wessex, is recorded as paying geld [land tax] of ten shillings. Although the name Ayshford has been unchanged since the Middle Ages it has, in common with most former Saxon communities, altered over time. *The Place Names of Devon* [3] gives its Saxon name in 958 as *Escford* but in a later charter dated 1027 this had changed to *Aescforda*. In Folio 112 of the *Exchequer Domesday* it is given as *Aisseford* with other documents listing the manor as *Aiseforda* and in 1238 as *Esseford*. Ayshford, to give it the name by which it is known today, was of considerable importance being one of four tithings in the parish of *Burdelescomb* (now Burlescombe), part of the Halberton hundred or wappentake, within which Ayshford and Westleigh were the two largest communities.

Prior to the Conquest the property had been owned by Wulfweard[4], a Saxon thane of whom little is known. By 1086 it was part of a much larger estate that extended from Instow and Iddesleigh in West Devon to Buckland and Churchstow in the South Hams, but was primarily centred on the Mid-Devon manor of Burlescombe. Following William's Cornubian campaign in 1068 that incorporated Devon and Cornwall into his kingdom, all these manors had been granted to one of his loyal followers, Walter de Claville. The majority of these farm holdings and manorial estates, including Burlescombe, were recorded as being held by him, but he appointed Osbern, Ansfrid and Riculf to manage three of his smaller West Devon properties and Walter was made responsible for West Raddon and Washford Pyne, two hill farms north of Crediton. Although this latter holding was assessed at one hide less one ferling and two parts of one virgate, which may in total be equated to about 100 acres, the land was clearly of little value being altogether rated for the sum of only nine shillings. Walter was a common name and neither of these holdings is shown as being managed by 'Walter the Steward'. Nevertheless, as both properties ended up in his care, it must be assumed that he is the same member of Walter de Claville's household, who was appointed as resident bailiff or manager for three other properties adjacent to the manorial estate of Burlescombe. Appointment as House Steward for a major landowner would usually be accompanied by the grant of an extended lease for a suitable local estate and Ayshford was one of Walter de Claville's principal holdings. Thus, apart from his domestic duties, Walter the House Steward's primary responsibility was for the manor of Ayshford, together with two small 50 acre farms to the north of Uplowman, Murley and Coombe.

The Exon version of Domesday provides more detail than is apparent from the millennium translation of the Exchequer copy, as it states that Walter's holding was in demesne [household of the Lord of the Manor]:
'On the day King Edward [the Confessor] was alive and dead it rendered geld for one hide.

This can be ploughed by 3 ploughs. Walter the House Steward holds this of him. Of it Walter has in demesne half a hide and one plough and the villans have half a hide and two ploughs. There Walter has 4 villans and 7 bordars [manorial tenants occupying farmsteads or dwellings within the hamlet] and 3 serfs and one packhorse and fourteen head of cattle and two swine and thirty-three goats and two brood mares and 12 acres of wood and 12 acres of meadow and 60 acres of pasture, and it is worth twenty shillings and was worth ten shillings when he [Walter] received it. Formerly 10 shillings; now it is worth 20 shillings.'[5]

No records survive that can establish a transfer of title of the Lordship of the manor of Burlescombe from Walter de Claville, whose family died out in about 1370[6], but according to Lysons[7] 'having been for some time litigated, it was in 1398 allotted [by Richard II] to Richard Warre, as one of the heirs of Sir Henry Percehay, baron of the Exchequer. About the year 1600 it was sold by Richard Warre of Hestercombe to Henry Ayshford from whom it has descended to William Ayshford Sanford' and subsequently by direct descent to the current Lord of the Manor, Edward William Ayshford Sanford.

The first official account that establishes the relationship between the Ayshford family and the manorial holding of the same name is in 1160 when it is recorded that Stephen de Esseford of *Esseford* gave land at Ayshford and Pugham[8] to the newly founded Abbey at *Leigh-Canonicorum* (now Canonsleigh).[9] Since this land formed part of Walter de Claville's estate in 1086, it is assumed that Stephen's father acquired Ayshford and several other de Claville properties[10] as a dowry, when he married one of Walter de Claville's daughters. A note by the local historian Roger Thorne in the Burlescombe Parish records in the Tiverton Library states that the forebear of the 'Esseford or Issford' family came over with the Conqueror and 'wandered the country until finally settling at Ayshford in the twelfth century', but there is no supporting evidence that can substantiate this premise. An alternative theory, raised by C.A.R. Radford in 1956[11], was that Stephen was the grandson of Walter the Steward, who had acquired the manor from de Claville and in accordance with accepted practice, had taken the name of Esseford (as it was known at the time) as his own. Stephen's ownership of other de Claville properties might have made this less likely except that recent research has shown that many of the household officers in baronial homes were hereditary positions brought across from Normandy or appointments given to junior or impoverished members of their family.

By the end of the 14th C the name of both manor and the family owning the estate had reverted to *Ayshford*; though for many a spelling of 'Airshford' would perhaps better reflect the modern Devon pronunciation of this hamlet. In 1609 Risdon recorded that 'Ashford in ancient evidences Esseford hath given name to a very ancient family, that from Stephanus de Esseford, not long after the conquest, flourish unto this day and are allied to many worthy houses. I read in an old roll, Johannes de Ashford habet villam de Ashford: and villa implies a court-house or chief place in the lord's manor.[12]' Whatever their origins, the Ayshfords were an ancient family who continued to live at Ayshford until 1662 when, following the death of Henry Ayshford, the last of the direct male line, the estate passed to his cousin Arthur Ayshford, and on his brother John's death in 1690, to their cousin John Sanford. Verification of the pedigree of the Lords of Ayshford (see Appendix 1) was provided by the extensive Ayshford archive inherited by the Sanford family in 1690, including fragments of an elaborate 17th C genealogical tree, and from the detailed researches undertaken on behalf of the surviving Ayshford family by Heather Ayshford.[13]

In the early part of the 13th C the family could best be described as landed farmers, owning or leasing well in excess of 700 acres of land to which the manor of Ayshford was central. Over the following three centuries they accumulated property throughout Devon and Somerset, primarily through marriage, and a position of considerable influence in Devon society. In about 1235 Stephen's great grandson John de Esseford married Agnes Peverel, the only child of Sir William Peverel of Sampford Peverell, bringing Peverel lands as her dowry. Following Sir William's death ca. 1240 this was challenged by the Peverel family as being entailed[14] in the male line. Most of these dowry holdings were eventually returned, but by an agreement dated 1262, the land called Gosmere [Goldsmore Farm near Trumps Cross on the road between Sampford Peverell and Westleigh] was acknowledged as having been acquired by her father himself; it was therefore not subject to the entail and her eldest son John Ayshford was allowed to retain it as part of his Ayshford estate. Agnes Ayshford is known to have lived to a great age, well over eighty years - seeing her great grandson John become Lord of Ayshford. Her name can be seen in the Testa de Nevill as the 'grande dame' responsible for payment to Reginald de Valla Torta of the Honour of Hurbeton [Halberton Hundred] of a one third fee for the manor of Ayshford.[15] Shortly before her son's death in 1283, John Ayshford made an agreement with the Prior of Canonsleigh that in return for a stated fee one of their priests would undertake duties at Ayshford Chapel. Although this is not the chapel that can be seen in the field beside the canal, it is the first mention of a private Ayshford family chapel. The recent restoration of Saint Michael's Chapel by Friends of Friendless Churches confirmed previously reported evidence of early mediaeval and late Norman stonework, which indicated that, although this building was almost certainly built in the early 15th C, probably by William Ayshford (ca.1361-1420), material had been used from a much older building.[16]

Further consolidation of the Ayshford estate had been achieved in about 1269, when John Ayshford's son Simon married Sarah, daughter and heiress to his neighbour Walter Botes, her dowry adding *Legh*, a property adjacent to Canonsleigh and Westleigh.[17] Twenty or so years later, his grandson's marriage to Margaret Woodford, heiress of Gilbert Crispin, brought the first holding of what would become a substantial estate in the South Hams, *Lamside in Holbeton* in the Erme valley south of Ivybridge. Apparently this property was also subject to an entail, but was bought off in 1320/21 by John Ayshford for the considerable sum of £100.[18]

John was clearly a wealthy landed farmer by this time as in 1306 he was able to afford to quitclaim[19] to the Abbess of Canonsleigh his rights to the land she held in the manor of Ayshford. Canonsleigh, to the foundation of which his forebear Stephen de Esseford had been a signatory, had in 1284 been 'increased in livelihood by Matilda de Clare, Countess of Gloucester and Hertford'[20] as a religious house for women. The Priory had not been sufficiently well endowed so the Prior and his canons were discharged and controversially replaced by an Abbess and canonesses. Some 60 years later in 1345 the Ayshford connection was recognised by the appointment of John Ayshford's grand-daughter Juliana Lamprey as Abbess. Another well known local Domesday manorial estate Morston [Mawston Barton near Cullompton] features briefly in the family tree with the marriage in 1360 of his grandson John to Edith Gambon, but the Black Death, which returned in 1361, was no respecter of age or wealth and he died in 1362 leaving a year old son William as heir to the Ayshford estates and subject to the Royal Courts of Wards.

Heather Ayshford describes this situation that affected infant heirs of landowners holding property of the King as a 'black hole'. All property held by the child's father was 'taken into the King's hands by the County Escheator [Royal Manager] to "safeguard" the infant heir's interests' with all estate revenues, less an allowance to support the child, going into the Royal coffers. Unsurprisingly, 'this arrangement was very popular with Kings and disliked by the nobility. William was in the hands of royal officials until July 1364 when the King [Edward III] granted custody of the lands to Henry Percehay at the yearly rent of £2.13s.4d (£750). The King would often keep the property of high born heirs for as long as possible, but with less wealthy subjects the rights would be sold off to the highest bidder. …William as a child would know nothing of this but Percehay's next move, in October 1377, would have much more of an impact. For the sum of £11.13s.4d (£4000) the King [Richard II] granted him the marriage of the heir. A ward of court could only marry with the King's permission and to a person chosen by the King. This was the right sold to Percehay. Many a wealthy man with an unmarried daughter used this route to gain socially superior in-laws. It was a way rich merchants could ensure that their grandchildren would be members of the nobility …though we do not know if William's eventual wife was the choice of Percehay.

The next hurdle [for a ward of court] was the proof of age. William had to show he was 21 and adult in order to regain his lands and his independence. …On Monday 30 March 1383, before John Ashton the Escheator of Devon, a long list of tenants and friends were produced by William to prove his age. Walter Gambon [of Mawston] said that he had a son born at Ayshford on 31 August 1361 after the birth of William and "saw the said William being suckled by his mother immediately after the birth". Roger Polford said he held a burning taper at the subsequent baptism, Thomas Jordan said his sister had been buried on the same day as the birth and her name was written in the missal [Service Book for the year], John Holm married Joan Grede in the chapel of St. Michael at Ayshford on the same day, and so on for a total of 13 witnesses. This constituted a grand jury and proved the case (and) William succeeded to his inheritance.

The family had survived a very risky period; with very high infant mortality William had been lucky to survive.'[21]

Although William married well, to Joan the daughter and co-heir of Robert

Wollavington of *Wollavington* in Somerset, thereby doubling his estate income, it was their son William by his marriage to Emma Ferrars, who was able to establish the family as one having the wealth and status to be of major influence in Devon. Emma was one of two daughters of William Ferrars of *Churston* [Churston Ferrers near Brixham] a wealthy landowner and Sheriff of Devon in 1396. In 1428 his estate was divided between Emma Ayshford and her sister Joan Yard. Her share of the properties, which may be seen in a superbly illustrated manuscript in the Somerset Record Office, increased their income six-fold and provided an estate that extended over three counties. Their son, another William, and grandchildren extended their family's noble connections with marriages to the Cary, Paulet and Wadham families and their great grandson Nicholas Ayshford Esquire (1485-1557) was one of the pallbearers for Princess Katherine, Countess of Devon and daughter of King Edward IV at her funeral at Tiverton on 2nd December 1527. His position in society as Lord of Ayshford, with an impressive Coat of Arms (Fig.1), was enhanced by the grant of royal franchise to hold Courts Leet, giving him criminal as well as manorial jurisdiction. Rolls survive in the family archive for Courts Leet held at Ayshford in 1520 and 1521 and for some of the Ayshford Courts Baron that continued until 1635.

Figure 1. Ayshford Coat of Arms: believed to have originally been placed over the door to the Ayshford aisle in Burlescombe Parish Church and later on the wall of Nynehead Court; now in the possession of the Ayshford Sanford family (Neil MacDonald)

The transformation of Ayshford Court from mediaeval timber building to the Tudor hall house that can be seen today was probably started around the turn of the century by his father William, but it is with Nicholas Ayshford and his grandson Roger that the rebuilding of this house and refurbishment of its chapel are most closely associated. With his wife Isabella, Nicholas also built the north (Ayshford) aisle of the Parish Church dedicated to St. Mary the Virgin at Burlescombe. His brightly decorated tomb (Fig.2) was erected in the sanctuary, but it is apparently empty and his grave may be seen in the floor of the Ayshford aisle.

Roger was over 50 years old, a good age for a man with a young family, and had been living at the property he had inherited from his mother, Culver House in Payhembury, when he came into the Ayshford estate. He added the south wing to the Court and was closely involved in local affairs, being an executor of the will of Peter Blundell, the founder of Blundell's School in Tiverton. He died in 1611 at the age of 77 and is buried at Burlescombe, where there is a monument on the wall of the Ayshford aisle dedicated to his memory and to that of his first

Figure 2. Nicholas Ayshford (1507-1585) sarcophagus tomb in the sanctuary of Burlescombe Parish Church
(Neil MacDonald)

Figure 3. Roger Ayshford (1537-1611) and his wife Elizabeth, daughter of Richard Michel of Pericourt: monument in the north-east corner of the Ayshford Aisle in Burlescombe Parish Church
(Neil MacDonald)

wife Elizabeth (Fig.3). In 1599 their elder son Henry (Fig.4) had married Amy Bluett (Fig.5), the daughter of Richard Bluett Esquire of Holcombe Court. Almost immediately Henry Ayshford set out to establish himself as one of the principal personalities in Devon. In 1600, as previously noted, Lysons recorded that Henry purchased the Lordship of Burlescombe from 'his cousin Ware' [Richard Warre of Hestercombe] and some eighteen years later added the manor and its estate for the sum of £3,400 (£420,000). In 1604 he had purchased the Prebend of Uffculme, giving him the right to appoint the Curate and to receive the income from Church lands and in 1616 his younger brother Thomas purchased the tithes of Burlescombe. However, his greatest expense was yet to come. In 1631 his eldest son Arthur married Lady Elizabeth Wilmot, daughter of the Rt. Hon. Charles Lord Wilmot, Viscount of Athlone and General Officer Commanding His Majesty King Charles' forces in the Kingdom of Ireland: the decorated ceiling and coving in the Elizabethan Wing 'Court Room' that was created in their honour being but a minor expenditure for this high society wedding. On 23rd June 1632 in a post-nuptial settlement, Henry granted his heir the Ayshford and Honington manorial estates, Great and Little Okenburne Farms, together with an annuity for life for Elizabeth to be charged on Ayshford Barton. Unfortunately within three years she had died; at her age of 23, it was probably in childbirth. After the death of her husband in the Civil War, a monument in their joint memory was placed on the north wall of the Ayshford

Figure 4. Henry Ayshford (1576-1650)
(Neil MacDonald)

aisle in Burlescombe Church (Fig.6). Arthur remarried almost immediately, but within two years his second wife had also died and both he and his father were now anxiously seeking an heir. In 1639 Arthur married Elizabeth Chudleigh, who in 1640/41 produced the long-desired heir Henry and his sister Elizabeth.

Arthur's brother, Henry's second son John, and their sister Mary, who married Henry Sanford of Nynehead, were also in receipt of generous post nuptial settlements. The deeds, written in April 1637, relating to the marriage between these two highly influential families, established Henry and Mary Sanford with holdings across Devon, Dorset and Somerset that included Culmstock, Clayhanger, Nynehead, Milverton and Langford, Winsford and Withypool, and ample resources to ensure their financial independence.[22]

Meanwhile, Henry Ayshford's career had continued to flourish; in 1632 he had been elected Devon's High Sheriff, in 1633 made Lieutenant Colonel in Colonel Francis Courtenay's

Figure 5. Amy Ayshford, daughter of Richard Bluett of Holcombe Court, married Henry Ayshford 1599, died 1659
(Neil MacDonald)

Figure 6. Arthur Ayshford (1601-ca. 1645) and his first wife Elizabeth, daughter of Lord Charles Wilmot, Viscount Athlone: monument on the north wall of the Ayshford aisle in Burlescombe Parish Church (Neil MacDonald)

Regiment and in 1638 appointed Deputy Lieutenant of Devon. Like most of the landed gentry the Ayshfords were convinced Royalists and in 1642, when Charles I established his Oxford Parliament, Henry was named as Commissioner of Array under the Earl of Bath, to raise militia forces in the King's name in Devon. Although declining field command, he signed the letter of 12 September 1644 to the War Council and was present when the King arrived in Exeter later that month. Henry remained in Exeter throughout the siege and attended the surrender of the City to General Fairfax at Poltimore in April 1646. His estates were compounded, but in Letters Patent, issued in November 1647, Henry was pardoned for his 'delinquency' in supporting the King; he was allowed to retain his estates, subject to a payment to Parliament of £1150 (£115,000). However, this was not his only penalty, for the Civil War had claimed the life of his eldest son and heir. Arthur had been a signatory to the Protestation[23] in 1641/2 and took a more active part in the Royalist campaign, but strangely, there is no record of his death, which had occurred before 1647 when his father rewrote his will. Apart from the memorial tablet for Elizabeth Wilmott in his Parish Church of Burlescombe on which his image also appears but is undated, there are no records or letters that have survived to shed light on this mystery.

Henry was determined to safeguard his inheritance and that of his grandson and entailed his estate to his own heirs with primacy to the male line, which effectively disinherited any surviving Ayshfords from previous generations. Within three years he was dead and his nine year old grandson Henry and his sister Elizabeth were in the guardianship of their grandfather Sir George Chudleigh, with an income of £200/year for Henry and a further £40 for his sister. Young Henry survived long enough to achieve his majority and to marry Lady Margaret Acland, the widow of Sir John Acland, but there were no children and the estate passed to his cousin Arthur, eldest son of his father's brother John. In 1661 Arthur had married Grace, daughter of John Courtenay of Molland, but their only child Henry died in 1666 aged 21 months, so when Arthur died three years later at the age of 29, the estate passed to the last of the entailed male line of the Ayshford family, his brother John.

Throughout this time the Court was barely used; the inventory of 1669 compiled after Arthur's death, showed that he and his wife Grace had occupied only three of the rooms, spending most of the time at their house in London.

Arthur's brother John had never been expected to inherit and had been apprenticed as a cloth merchant. Having completed his apprenticeship, he established his own highly successful business in London, trading primarily with Hamburg in Germany. He remained a bachelor until he was nearly 30, when he married Susanna, the second daughter of fellow entrepreneur Lucius Knightly, whose eldest daughter Elizabeth had married John's cousin (and potentially his heir) John Sanford of Nynehead. John and Susanna eventually established themselves at Ayshford Court but, unlike her sister, for Susanna there were to be no children. Heather Ayshford records that Liz and Cliff Watson, who were tenants of Ayshford Court's south wing in the 1980s, would always remember 'hearing a woman sobbing which they always associated with Susanna crying over the loss of a baby'. Whether these ghostly tears were related to Susanna's death (puerperal fever was very common) is not known, but she was buried in the chapel at Ayshford in December 1688. John survived her for just over a year and was buried beside his wife in March 1690. His will written in January 1689, two copies of which, together with the other documents, can be seen in the Somerset Record Office[24], made 'John Sanford formerly Member of Parliament for Taunton and now for Minehead' his sole heir. He also made generous provision for the repair of the chapel, his chaplain and steward and the poor and his surviving Ayshford relations. His estate included a large library, predominantly religious books and those relating to his business interests in Europe, but surprisingly, despite his own success and inherited wealth, he had apparently needed to sell much of the family silver, the sale in May 1688 realising the sum of £120 5s 0d (£12,000). The inventory of his property dated 9 May 1690 was made out by John Sanford's clerk and became the subject of some strong criticism from Sanford's neighbour, Edward Clarke of Chipley. He was clearly a close friend of Nicholas Ayshford, on behalf of whom he wrote a long and detailed letter to John Sanford and his co-executors stating in no uncertain terms that they were 'undervaluing the goods mentioned in the inventory, every particular thereof being really and truly verie much undervalued to the greater prejudice of Mr Nicholas Ayshford, who by the wyll is to have an estate for his life. There were several things of great value, jewellery plate, etc. totally left out of the inventory...' Edward Clarke also copied this letter to the other beneficiaries, presumably to ensure that his letter could not be ignored. Unfortunately the response was not preserved, though a letter from Nicholas Ayshford to Edward Clarke dated 29 June provides evidence of other omissions.[25]

Henry Ayshford's entail had ensured that the estate would pass to his daughter Mary's son[26] but, as can be seen from the Ayshford family tree, three other lines survived of which two remain in the male line to this day. For Henry's family, the line was continued by his daughter, whose marriage to Henry Sanford (Fig.7) in 1637 would, some fifty years later, combine the estates of the two most important families of landed gentry in this part of the south-west. Over the next two centuries it would provide the Sanford (later to become the Ayshford Sanford) family with great

Figure 7. Henry Sanford (1612-1644) of Nynehead; married to Mary Ayshford (1607-1662) in 1637
(Neil MacDonald)

wealth and influence in the highest echelons of society[27] (See Appendix 2). Family legend has it that the combined Ayshford and Sanford estates of well over 5,000 acres allowed them to ride from Taunton to Exeter on their own land, although the intervening Acland estate at Killerton makes this assertion somewhat apocryphal. Nevertheless, they were now landowners in the top rank of Georgian society. Originally from Winsford on the Devon/Somerset border, Martin Sanford had acquired Nynehead circa 1599. He became High Sheriff of Somerset in 1641 and together with his son Henry declared his allegiance to Parliament. With her father and father-in-law on opposing sides, this must have been a difficult time for Mary (Ayshford) that was compounded by the deaths in 1643 and 1644 of her father-in-law Martin and her husband Henry and, at about the same time, of her brother Arthur. She had previously lost her eldest son Martin and as none of his sons had survived, the Sanford estate passed to her second son John. He, like his cousin John Ayshford, was also a London cloth merchant dealing primarily with Holland and Germany, but returned to Somerset to take over his estate. In 1675 he initiated a major rebuilding programme for Nynehead and between 1685 and 1699 was successively MP for Taunton and Minehead. His inheritance of the Ayshford family estates in 1690 was hedged by trusteeship over a period of 159 years. Whilst John Sanford would have all rights to the estate for 60 years, the income and control of the property would then pass to Nicholas Ayshford (eldest son of Roger Ayshford's second son Thomas) and his heirs for the succeeding 99 years. In the event, in June 1700, Nicholas released his rights to John Sanford in return for the payment of £3000 (£360,000) part of which was used to found and endow the Uffculme Grammar School.[28] Nicholas Ayshford died in 1701 and is buried in the Ayshford aisle at Burlescombe.

Until the Ayshford Court estate was sold to a local investor, Charles Home-Smith, in the mid 1930s, it remained in the possession of the Ayshford Sanford family, but they continued to live at Nynehead (Fig.8) in Somerset and the Devon property was let to a succession of tenants. Many of these lease agreements, primarily from the 18th and 19th C, can be seen in the Sanford papers. Some of these documents include a detailed description of the house and farm buildings. On 5th December 1730 the Court was leased by Anne Sanford of Nynehead [acting for her son William Sanford, who was a minor aged 13 at the time] 'to William Corner of Ayshford yeoman for 7 years for part of barton of Ayshford comprising kitchen, workmen's hall, cellar adjoining, larder next kitchen, dairy, brewhouse, malthouse, chambers over same (except the broad chamber), barn, place under the wayne house, upper new built stable and shippon with liberty for Henry [Woolcott, cordwainer who held the lease for the grist mill] to make cider in the pound house for his own use and put apples in pound house chamber, part of barton house Ayshford, wood court, hoggs styes, crib house in Boobery, hopyard, gardens (except nursery enclosed next highway), young orchard formerly Barley Meade, the Higher Garden, the Mill Garden, Higher and Lower Bartis, Pugham Down, Aysbeare Meadow, 3 Hay Crofts, Long Downe, Long Meadow, Bowbrey, (sic) Roditch, Leverlands, 2 Leighs, Horse Leigh, Great Court Meadow, Park Wood new pasture and great tithes of Ayshford for £206 rent'.[29] In 1706 and 1713 almost identical seven year leases had been given to Henry Hewett of Nynehead and John Harward, also of Nynehead, but both excluded the 'newly built stable and shippon', which shows that the Sanfords were maintaining and investing in the commercial parts of their property from an early stage. Further improvements to these farm buildings were undertaken by John Sanford's grandson William Sanford, who served as High Sheriff of Somerset in 1743, removing or renovating the last of the old wooden structures and replacing them with cob and stone barns. However, Davidson in his *Notes on Devon Churches*,[30] states that 'the mansion, after the death of the last heir male in 1689 (sic), was dismantled and now, 1828, only the inferior offices are standed', which implies that although the farm buildings that made up the outer courtyard were being improved the wooden buildings that still made up much of the inner courtyard were removed.

In 1779 William Ayshford Sanford, who was the first member of the family to add Ayshford to his name, succeeded to the estate at the age of seven. Nynehead being

Figure 8. Nynehead Court from an engraving dated 1792 (Nynehead & District Local History Society)

apparently tenanted at the time, he was brought up in London, but following his marriage he returned to his family home. He was clearly conscious of local social problems for, as the Nynehead history records, 'William was well aware of the distress caused by the agricultural depression after the Napoleonic Wars and actively campaigned for social and economic improvements. He provided work for local men by remodelling the parkland at Nynehead Court'[31] (Fig.9) and building new barns at Ayshford. He also built two small extensions to the Court that included the provision of modern sanitation, and restored the Ayshford Chapel windows. It is not clear if it was William Ayshford Sanford or his father, who removed the old wooden cupola above the west door of the chapel and built the present bell-cote (Fig.10) in its place, but it seems more likely to have been a turn of the 18-19th C addition.

In 1768 his grandfather William Sanford had been involved with the group of Taunton men, who had instructed Mr James Brindley to survey for a canal from the Tone to the Exe, as the line would of necessity pass through his land at Nynehead. The purpose of this canal was to complete a link for cargo, primarily coal from South Wales, to the English Channel that would avoid the dangers of the Lands End peninsula. Although this survey had been completed by Robert Whitworth in 1769, it came to naught. It was revived in 1792 and four years later on 24 March 1796 *'An Act making a Navigable Canal from the River Exe near the Town of Topsham to the River Tone near the Town of Taunton'* was approved by Parliament. Various

Figure 9. Nynehead Court garden in the late 19th century (Nynehead & District Local History Society)

factors contributed to a delay in starting work, but the renewal of hostilities with France in July 1797 forced its sponsors to abandon the project. Ten years later interest in the canal was revived. William Ayshford Sanford was not a subscriber to the Grand Western Canal Company, but became closely involved in negotiations in 1808-10, as the route of the canal passed through both his Nynehead and Ayshford estates. These negotiations culminated in the Act of 1811 and a compensation payment of £6000 (£292,500) for the loss of his land and access during the canal's construction. This second Navigation Act altered the route of the canal through his Burlescombe and Ayshford estate 'in a certain Mead called Mear Wood Great Meadow otherwise Clist Meadow, in the Parish of Burlescombe in the said County of Devon, belonging to William Ayshford Sanford Esquire, into and through the villages of Ashford (sic) and Sampford Peverell ...' [32].

Figure 10. Ayshford Chapel Bell-cote, probably added ca. 1800 by William Ayshford Sanford (1772-1833) (Apex Photo Agency)

Designed to avoid the centre of Halberton, the new route was at a higher level, which required construction of an embankment to carry the canal above the village of Ayshford but had the advantage of reducing the number of properties that would have to be destroyed. Work started on the canal's Tiverton spur from Lowdwells in 1810 and was completed in 1814, but it was to be another 24 years before the link to Taunton was achieved. By the 1840s the canal was in direct competition with the railway and having no link to the English Channel, trade inevitably declined. The Taunton link was closed in 1867 and the Tiverton –Lowdwells length that had remained operational for stone traffic was closed in 1962.[33] Unfortunately construction of the embankment dominated the village of Ayshford and so changed the environs of the Court that, as Davidson wrote in 1828, 'the antient approaches to the Buildings are destroyed by the grand western canal which bisects the Lands';[34] the present road and back entrance to the Court was constructed in its place, but its view across the vale of the Lyner to the Blackdown Hills was spoiled for ever. William Ayshford Sanford was succeeded by his son Edward in 1833. He served as MP for Taunton from 1830-41, High Sheriff of Somerset in 1848, Chairman of the Quarter Sessions, Deputy Lieutenant and was elected a Fellow of the Royal Society. Like his father he was a concerned landlord and undertook further improvements to his property on behalf of his tenants. Between 1847 and 1860 he undertook a major restoration of Ayshford Chapel, extended the west wing of the Court and added several buildings to the outer courtyard, including the barn that now makes up its southern side, but these were the last major changes. Ayshford was now peripheral to the Ayshford Sanford estate that was centred on Nynehead; over the next eighty years only routine maintenance and repairs were undertaken. In the words of the well known Devon historian WG Hoskins, it had become a 'diminished farmhouse' and was sold. The Lordship of Ayshford continued to appear in the wills of successive members of the Ayshford Sanford family until 1793; thereafter it seems to have been subsumed into the Lordship of Burlescombe, a title retained by the present Edward William Ayshford Sanford.

In the late 1930s the Ayshford estate, which was still well in excess of 2,000 acres, was divided. The Ayshford Court farm estate of around 400 acres was sold to Charles Home-Smith in 1938 and the Burlescombe properties were auctioned by John Woods in 1939. With the threat of war looming over an already depressed market, prices were low and some farms had to be sold privately. The Boehill estate of 140 acres was retained in trust for a further 15 years before being sold to improve the trust's income, leaving the chapel field and the Chapel of Saint Michael as the only part of the Ayshford estate still in the family's possession. Although leased to the Friends of Friendless Churches for 125 years, it is a matter of great pride for the Ayshford Sanford family that this small building and the land on which it stands remains their property and so retains their link with the Conquest and their Ayshford inheritance.

---

[1] Hooke, D. *Pre-Conquest Charter-Bounds of Devon and Cornwall*, Woodbridge, Suffolk 1994 pp 156-160.

[2] The 'hide' had several meanings at this time, but it is described in the OED as the extent of land that can be tilled by one plough in a year that may be equated to 100 acres of cultivated land. A 'virgate' is a lesser measure that is usually taken as being about 30 acres.

[3] *The Place Names of Devon* by JEB Gover, A Mawer and FM Stenton, Cambridge University Press 1932. The name Ayshford would usually mean 'ford by the ash trees', but can also be understood to be the 'road by the ash trees'.

[4] According to *Exon Domesday* his name was Olvard.

[5] The description of this holding differs slightly in the Exchequer version being 12 acres of pasture, 60 acres of meadow and 12 acres of woodland – the significance of 'pasture' when compared with 'meadow' is unclear and may only be in the mind of the translator.

[6] The Ayshford family were briefly re-united with the de Claville's in 1343 when John Ayshford (ca. 1329-1362) married Joan de Claville, but she died without issue and he subsequently married Edith Gambon.

[7] Lysons, D. and S. *Magna Britannia vi, Topographical and Historical Account of Devonshire* (2 vols) London 1822 Vol 2 pp 91-3

[8] Worth, RN. *A History of Devonshire*, Elliot Stock, London 1886.

[9] This ecclesiastical benefice had been provided by William de Claville, Lord of Burlescombe during the reign of Henry II (1154-1189) for a Prior and Austin Canons, but during the reign of Edward I (1272-

1309) it was further endowed by Maud de Clare, Countess of Gloucester and Hertford and converted to a Nunnery with an Abbess and Canonesses of the same order. At the time of the Dissolution in 1536 it was assessed at £197, marginally under the limit of £200 imposed by Parliament for dissolution, and closed. It was leased by Henry VIII for 21 years to Thomas de Soulemont and subsequently sold by Elizabeth I to Sir George St. Leger.

[10] The other properties included Upton Pyne, which remained in the possession of the Ayshford and Ayshford Sanford families until the mid 1700s.

[11] Radford, CAR. *'Ayshford Court, Burlescombe'; Devon & Cornwall Notes & Queries* 27 (1956-58) pp 196-98.

[12] Risdon, T. *The Geographical Description or Survey of the County of Devon.* Although written at the start of the reign of James I, it was not published until 1811 and was then extensively quoted by Polwhele, Lysons and other historians.

[13] Ayshford, F&H. *Notes towards a history of the Ayshford family of Devon.* The Sandford MSS was acquired by Somerset County Council in 2001 and has been a particularly valuable source of mediaeval and renaissance material.

[14] Entail – to settle land or an estate on a number of persons in succession so that it cannot be dealt with by any one possessor as absolute owner. *QED*

[15] Testa de Nevill is the assessment of Knight's fees payable to the Court of the Exchequer of the King [Henry III and subsequently Edward I] for the whole of England. Devon section transcribed in *Transactions of the Devonshire Association Vol.30.* 1898 pp.203-37 stated to relate to the end of the reign of Edward I (1272-1307).

[16] The use of Norman and early mediaeval stonework in the building of the chapel had been previously reported by F. Bond Bligh in 1912 in an article entitled 'Ayshford Chapel and Manor House' in the *Somersetshire Archaeological and Natural History Society Proceedings vol lvii*

[17] This property, known as Boteslegh, remained in the family for nearly 200 years until given by William Ayshford (1456-1608) in 1465 as part of his sister Florence's dowry to John Frances of Combe Florey for which he paid a nominal rent. Later known as Gwyns after the family who absorbed the Frances properties by marriage.

[18] For this and subsequent sterling conversions, the Lawrence H Officer and Samuel H Williamson calculator has been used. For the period 1320-1970 this equates to £40K or ten times this amount if taken to 2007 - see **www.measuringworth.com.**

[19] Quitclaim – make a formal renunciation of a right. *OED*. In this case for ground rents payable to him for land he had leased to Canonsleigh.

[20] Polwhele, Richard. *The History of Devonshire (3 vols)*, London 1793-1806 Vol 2 pp 367-68

[21] Ayshford, F&H. *Notes towards a history of the Ayshford family of Devon.*

[22] Somerset Record Office Sanford Estate documents *DD/SF/2/1/15-17*

[23] In an attempt to avert a civil war that no-one wanted, in July 1641 an Act of Parliament required all men over the age of 18 to sign the 'Protestation' pledging allegiance to both King and Church. This edict was passed from the Speaker through the High Sheriff and Justices of the Peace to every Parish Priest, who was required to proclaim the Protestation to his parishioners and send the signed returns back to Parliament. Although not intended as a census it is the earliest list of the population that survives.

[24] Somerset Record Office Sanford Estate documents *DD/SF11/1/100*

[25] Somerset Record Office Sanford Estate documents *DD/SF/7/1/15*

[26] Henry's sister Elizabeth survived him. She was left £1000 in his will 'to add to her already considerable fortune' but apparently she never married and had died before her cousin John wrote his will in 1689. No record can be located of her will or her place of burial.

[27] The history of this family, their principal residence, Nynehead Court and its community is included in *The Book of Nynehead* published for the Nynehead and District Local History Society. Halsgrove 2003

[28] Information relating to this bequest can be found in *Uffculme, a Peculiar Parish*, Uffculme Archive Group 1997

[29] Somerset Record Office Sanford Estate documents *DD/SF/2/70/19 and 2/70/66*. The list includes field names some of which survive but most have been lost due to enlargement for modern farming practice.

[30] Davidson, J.B. *Notes on Devon Churches – East Devon*, West Country Studies Library microfiche p.569

[31] *The Book of Nynehead* pp.33-35

[32] 51 Geo.III c.168. *An Act to vary and alter the Line of a Cut authorised to be made by an Act of the Thirty-sixth Year of His Present Majesty. For making a Canal from the River Exe, near Topsham in the County of Devon, to the River Tone, near the town of Taunton in the County of Somerset: and to amend the said Act.* Passed 15 June 1811.

[33] For a full description of the construction and running of this canal see Harris, H. *The Grand Western Canal*, David & Charles 1973

[34] Davidson, J.B. *Notes on Devon Churches – East Devon*, West Country Studies Library microfiche p.569

AYSHFORD COURT

None of the original Court buildings, which were almost certainly entirely constructed of wood, have survived. Even the existing buildings have to be treated with caution. As GW Copeland in his personal historical notes on Ayshford Court and its Chapel states 'that although the mediaeval documents clearly indicate the great antiquity of the site [this] should never, without very great caution, be ascribed to any building thereon, as in most cases a very great deal of rebuilding and re-modelling occurred periodically down the centuries until all vestiges of the earliest building on the site were completely obliterated, buried or swept away.'[1]

Ayshford Court in mediaeval times was described by Polwhele[2] as one of the finest houses in the West of England, but a declining founding family fortune and extinction of a direct lineal descent reduced its importance as a family seat. For the past 150 years it has been a farmhouse with its original estate of around 400 acres of pasture, arable and some woodland seemingly intact, but by the late 1970s all of the land, apart from the chapel field and a curtilage for the Court of just over an acre, had been sold as two separate farms: the former home farm, now known as Ayshford Court Farm, with most of its 232 acres above the canal between Holbrook and Westcott, and the former Bowdens, now known as Lower Ayshford Farm, on the remaining 168 acres below the canal and extending beyond the River Lyner to the main Exeter to London railway line. For the past 40 years the house has been occupied as a private dwelling but, with little maintenance being carried out, it continued to decay until 2003 when it was sold to a developer.

Figure 11. Ayshford Court - the Hall restored to expose its Tudor beams and open plan
(Neil MacDonald)

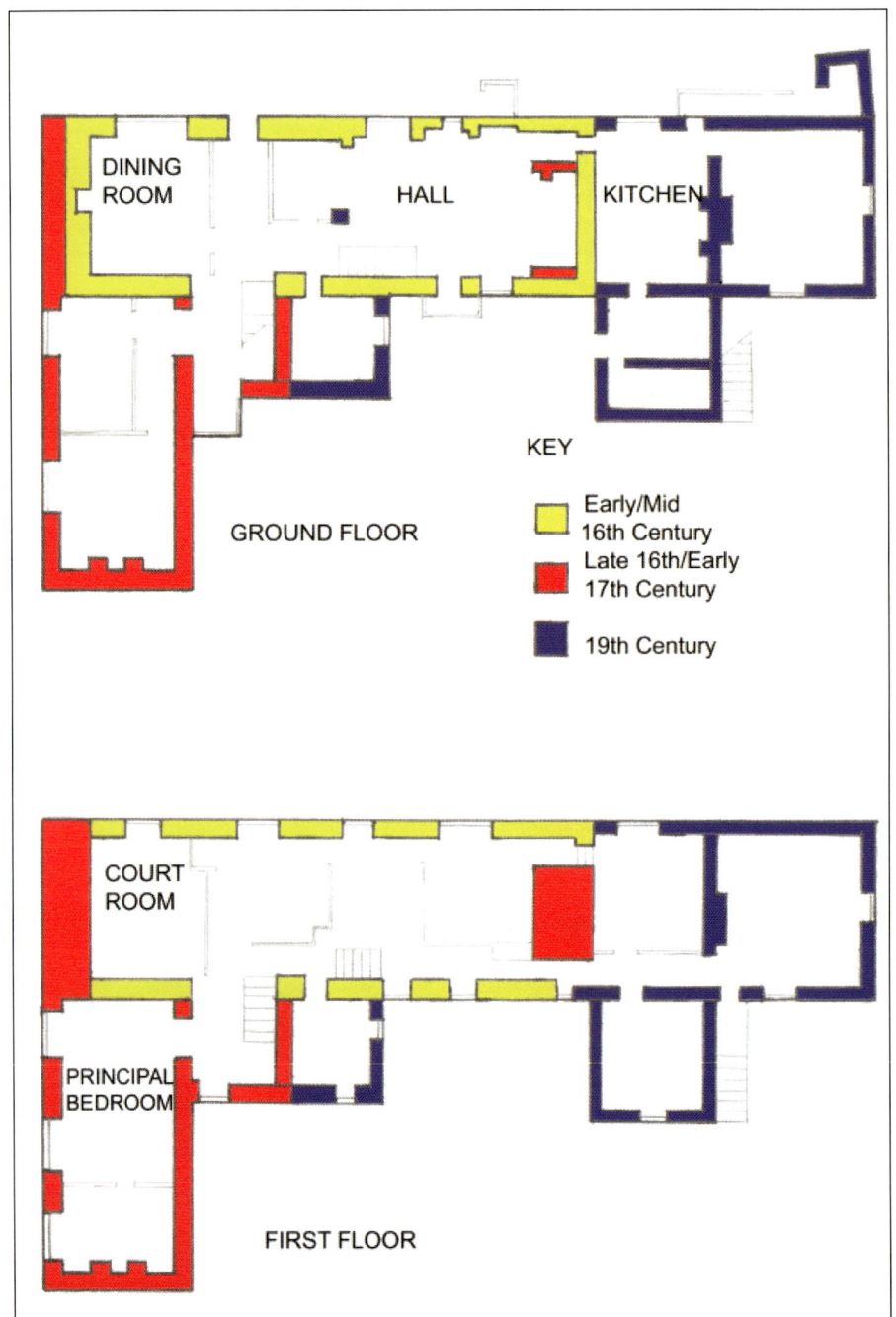

Figure 12. Ayshford Court - ground floor and first-floor plans

Extensively renovated and refurbished, the Court is now a comfortable family home (Fig.11). Although nothing survives of the mediaeval manor it is considered unlikely that the site and orientation of the original manorial buildings would be markedly different from those that can be seen today. The presence of a courtyard, albeit now incomplete, and of farm buildings with a central gatehouse leading into a second courtyard, likewise incomplete, is typical of many mediaeval manors. So although much reduced in size and grandeur, the stone and brick buildings that replaced the wooden structures from the 16th C onwards are still of considerable architectural interest and merit and are Grade II listed. However, all recorded studies of the architectural features of Ayshford Court have been complicated by a series of major additions and changes to the internal layout. The 19th C alterations dramatically altered the external appearance of the building and division of the property into two separate but conjoined dwellings during the 1939-45 war had an equally significant effect on the internal structure and layout. The description of the Court and its former farm buildings that follows owes much to Radford's notes that were published in 1956-58 and Copeland's observations in 1964, with allowance for the rooms created by the recent restoration. Removal of most internal 19th C and 20th C stud walling has ensured that much of this house is now probably closer to its Tudor and Stuart origins than it was some fifty years ago (Fig.12).

The Court, which faces south and west, has two wings; the earlier, but very much modified, western wing is opposite the former Gatehouse, with a small walled garden behind (Fig 13). Originally of traditional late mediaeval or Tudor hall-house

Figure 13. Ayshford Court - west wing from the walled garden (Neil MacDonald)

Figure 14. Detail - jointed cruck (Neil MacDonald)

plan, the house was almost certainly partly floored with a central hall and stairs leading to a solar or bedchamber, probably at the northern end, and servants' quarters on the southern side. The main, now slated, roof is of jointed cruck construction, as illustrated in Cherry and Pevsner's *Buildings in Devon*[3]; recent renovation has left many main timbers exposed and two of these jointed crucks (Fig.14) can be seen in the first floor passage above the central entrance door. Though Pevsner and Copeland put its earliest construction as mid or late 16th C, Radford believed that this western wing was much earlier. Dating the Court to circa 1500, he cited an original two-light rectangular oak-pegged window with ovolo[4] mould and sunken spandrels, which can be seen on the right-hand side of the former main entrance (Fig. 15 and 16): its low elevation confirming that it belonged to the hall[5]. Support for the open plan nature of the central hall of the original building was provided by soot deposits found on the underside of the main roof timbers during recent renovation, and this would also seem to endorse Radford's earlier dating. It is known Nicholas Ayshford, who succeeded his father William in 1508 and died in 1557, undertook major improvements to his house and probably the family chapel. This may well have included 'ceiling' the central hall[6] and constructing the west wing chimney with its large ingle-nook fireplace (Fig.17) and the remains of

Figure 15. Ayshford Court - west wing from the inner courtyard (Neil MacDonald)

Figure 16. Detail - two-light oak-pegged window (ca. 1500) (Neil MacDonald)

a traditional bread oven; the latter was probably destroyed in the Victorian period when the kitchen range was installed.

When Radford visited the farm in 1953 the house was divided with entry from the courtyard to the south wing, through a Victorian porch in the corner, and a central entrance to the west wing. Here the original entrance door had long since gone and the central doorway led into a passage, with a kitchen on the right and stairs leading to the first floor. Further partitions provided a passage to a dining room, with a door to the garden and to a sitting room beyond. The kitchen fireplace was blocked off, hidden behind a range, and, apart from three of the main oak beams, there was little visible evidence of the layout of the hall. Today it is entirely open. The six main oak beams that support the first floor rooms are totally exposed; the beam at the far end of the hall, which like the others originally extended across the full width of the house, was found in 2003 to have been cut back; its end propped up by a rather crude octagonal oak pillar. This alteration was almost certainly undertaken during William Ayshford Sanford's 19thC renovations to provide sanitary facilities

Figure 17. Hall - Ingle-nook fireplace   (Neil MacDonald)

Figure 18. Ayshford Court - Victorian porch and corner extension   (Neil MacDonald)

Figure 19. West wing - first floor passage (Neil MacDonald)

by constructing a brick extension to an existing 17thC annexe in the corner of the two wings (Fig.18). Access to the south wing from the hall is gained through an early 17thC two-centred oak doorway in the south-east corner. This leads to a passage that crosses the house from the south wing porch to the garden and to two staircases, the former 19thC narrow back stairs in a corner of the hall to the west wing landing and a broad access staircase to the south wing that was repositioned in 2003.

On the first floor the longitudinal passage, which used to run on the western side, has been moved across so that all west wing bedrooms now look out over the garden. Wherever possible timbers have been left exposed (Fig.19) and the ceiling of the central landing of this western wing can be seen to be supported by a large chamfered end-stopped oak beam. This wing has an early 19th C brick and stone extension on its northern side; slate slabs and drainage channels, now all removed, indicated its one-time use as a slaughter house and cold store. The attached similarly built extension in the north-east corner was added later, presumably by Edward Ayshford Sanford, who had succeeded his father in 1833, and probably provided the dairy and larder. This extension may well have been on the site of a wooden or cob building that would at one time have formed the northern side of the inner courtyard. The first floor lofts of both extensions were provided with access from an external flight of steps and were probably used for general storage (Fig.20). Of little architectural interest, these buildings have all been incorporated into the main house with access through the walls at both ground and first floor level.

Figure 20. Ayshford Court - west wing 19th century extensions (Neil MacDonald)

The earliest addition to the Court, always referred to by successive owners as the 'Elizabethan Wing' (Fig.21), was built of Westleigh stone at the turn of the 16/17th centuries by Nicholas Ayshford's grandson Roger Ayshford, who died in 1610. This date is again marginally earlier than the early 17thC attribution by Copeland and

Figure 21. Ayshford Court - 'Elizabethan' south wing from the canal　　　(Neil MacDonald)

Pevsner, but Radford was sure of its late 16th C construction stating that 'One of the rooms [principal bedroom] retains the original fireplace with a heavy moulded and stopped frame. The detail shows that the new range was built about 1600 and a reset stone, with the date 1594, probably marked the completion of the work.'[7] Unfortunately this evidence has either been covered up or removed, but the central south wing chimney stack with its band of quatrefoils below the cap-mould bears the inscription "Built 1607/ Rebuilt 1910". There are three original three-light mullioned rectangular stone windows with hood moulds on the south side of the first floor and one that has been rebuilt on the ground floor (Fig.22). All are certainly early 17th C and could well be slightly earlier. A former, probably matching, window was removed when the French windows were installed in the 1960s. There is another similar three-light stone mullioned window that looks onto the garden from the Hall on the ground floor of the west wing.

Access to this south wing was provided by a small square annexe in the corner of the two wings with a staircase to a landing on the upper floor, which probably replaced a circular stair that was usually found leading to the chamber above the hall of a mediaeval

Figure 22. Mullion window　　(Neil MacDonald)

Figure 23. South wing - principal bedroom fireplace and moulded plaster ceiling (ca. 1600)
(Neil MacDonald)

house. Prior to the recent restoration the staircase had been repositioned, but has now been returned to its original location facing the passage to the garden entrance. From the landing at the top of the stairs, a rectangular wooden-framed doorway leads into the principal bedroom with an elaborate plaster ceiling with partial frieze adorned with berries and thistles (Fig.23), the moulds for which, as Radford noted, 'had been designed for a larger room and the pattern does not fit the space'. In addition, the design only covers four-fifths of the ceiling, but as the position of the stone mullioned windows and the previously described fireplace are central to the room, and the wall to the room beyond is clearly original, it would seem likely that the ceiling was damaged at some time and the moulding not reinstated.

Off the staircase landing to the right of the stairs there are two early 17th C plainly-stopped rectangular wooden doorways; the right-hand door, closed off when the house was divided, provides access to the west wing; the left-hand door to another bedroom known as the 'Court Room' with an elaborate moulded and coved plaster ceiling (Fig.24). With the date 1631 it seems likely that this was undertaken by Henry Ayshford (1576-1650) at the time of his eldest son Arthur's first marriage to Elizabeth Wilmot, being as Radford describes it 'a suitable apartment for the eldest son of the house and his bride.' At a much later date the floor to this room was raised, possibly to give additional ceiling height to the room below; this gives the room a somewhat cramped appearance with its west-facing window at a lower level than usual. Together with the dining room below, it forms the junction between the two wings and here the south wall is of vast proportions being well over 2 metres thick. During the 2003 renovations the Victorian fireplace in the bedroom was removed and within the stack, some 50cms above mantel level, access to a priest's hole was revealed (Fig.25). The need for such a retreat within the home of this Anglican Devon family is a mystery and there were no relics within it to give any clues as to its use or its date. Presumably constructed either by Nicholas Ayshford in the reign of Mary I, or perhaps during the Civil War or Commonwealth period by Henry Ayshford, over time its existence was forgotten and its discovery was a complete surprise to historians and the Ayshford Sanford

Figure 24. South wing - Court Room fireplace, moulded ceiling and frieze   (Neil MacDonald)

family alike.

Structural problems, probably due in part to the different ceiling heights of the two wings and partial removal of the supporting beams, had over time severely distorted the south-west corner of the west wall. The eaves at this point had dropped noticeably and the oak-framed triple-light ground floor window was found to be in imminent danger of collapse. This would have brought down the entire wall and was only saved by inserting a stone pillar into the centre of the window, which now consists of two separate lights. Work in this area also involved stripping the old lime plaster from the passage wall to reveal an early 17th C oak screen, which has now been left uncovered. Unlikely to be in its original position, like the octagonal pillar on the other side of

Figure 25. Detail - Priest's hole in the Court Room chimney stack   (Neil MacDonald)

the passage, it was probably put in place during William Ayshford Sanford's work in the early 19th C.

Although the original hall could well have been thatched, it was certainly slated at an early date and the south wing has always had a hipped slate roof. In addition to the previously described early 17th C chimney stack in the centre of the south wing, there are two 17th C rectangular chimneys at either end of the west wing and one at the eastern end of the south wing. A further similar but 19th C chimney for the west wing extension now serves the modern kitchen.

It is hard to reconcile the 1841 Tithe map of the buildings that provided the outer courtyard (Fig.26) with those that are there today. This extensive range of outbuildings to the north and east of the Court was surveyed by Copeland in 1964; unfortunately over the last half century they have suffered major deterioration and two of them no longer exist. Brick and cob buildings with low hay-lofts are mostly incompatible with modern farming machinery and have had to be replaced with high roofed Dutch barns. The 1989 hurricane, combined with a general state of disrepair, virtually destroyed three more of these barns and only those on the southern and the western sides up to and including the Gatehouse are still in use. These too will need extensive work if they are to survive for much longer. Access to the outer courtyard through the Gatehouse (Fig.27) is still feasible, although the doors have been shut for over 30 years and the area is badly overgrown. As Copeland reported in 1964, this building 'has a wooden lintel to the rectangular passage... (and) within the passage are stone projections with chamfered edges on their east side and with rectangular recesses therein.'[8] Copeland provides no explanation for these curious shallow recesses; perhaps they were intended for lanterns or rush lights to illuminate the entrance to the inner courtyard. The upper part of the Gatehouse is brick with an attractive two-light oak-framed window, probably mid-18th C, overlooking the outer courtyard and the remains of the frame of a matching two-light window on the opposite side. Access to this upper level is

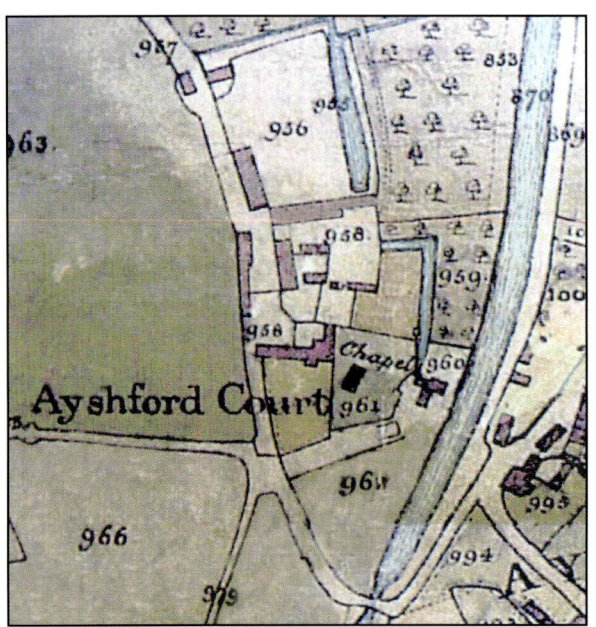

Figure 26. Extract from 1839 Tithe Commissioner's map of Devon (Devon Record Office)

provided by a door from the adjacent barn on the southern side.

The 'L' shaped barns, which provide half of the western and all of the southern sides of the outer courtyard, are of open timber construction on stone staddles or pillars (Fig.28). The roof was formerly slated but is now covered with galvanised iron sheeting. Most of the main floor beams, together with one of the pillars, were removed in the 1970s to give tractor access, but within living memory this vast space was close-boarded and regularly used for barn dances. A full carriage-width door at the eastern end provided access through the barn to the grist mill and chapel yard. As the south-facing long barn does not feature on the 1841 tithe map, it was almost certainly built by Edward Ayshford Sanford in the late 1850s. However the west-facing barn that adjoins the Gatehouse was described by Copeland as 'an open timber barn supported on a species of cruck, suggestive of quite early work; and it has wind braces' and is probably mid 18th C.

In the south-east corner of the courtyard is the ivy-clad remains of the largest building in this complex. It lost its roof in the hurricane and has since fallen into total disrepair, but hidden by ivy at the top of one of the remaining stone pillars is a plaque with the inscription 'REBUILT/?/1860'[9] that clearly ties in with other work undertaken by Edward Ayshford Sanford. This three-storied building, built on the foundations of an existing barn that formed the eastern side of the outer courtyard, was constructed as a water mill to replace the old water-powered grist mill that can be seen on the 1841 map below

Figure 27. Ayshford Court - Gatehouse leading from the outer to the inner courtyard (mid 18th century with earlier foundations) (Neil MacDonald)

Figure 28. Ayshford Court - outer courtyard, south barn (Neil MacDonald)

the chapel, but of which nothing now remains. Although the wheel, and virtually all other evidence relating to the barn's one time use, was removed in the late 1960s, the pit that contained the waterwheel can still be seen on its southern side. With no running streams near the property, water to power the mill was provided by an ingenious system of holding ponds that can be seen on the 1841 map, though all except two at the top of the farm have now been filled in. As these ponds were only replenished from field run off and drains, the mill was somewhat restricted in its use except during times of heavy winter rain. The final outflow from the millwheel pit was into an underground culvert constructed beneath the chapel field by the Canal Company to take excess rainwater from Brimstone Lane. This culvert, which can be accessed from a manhole in the hollow, passes under the canal to a ditch that runs at the side of the Holbrook-Westleigh road.

There is little, apart from foundations and a heap of rubble, that remains of the four other barns that once completed the outer courtyard; one on the eastern side, two adjacent barns on the northern side and a barn to the north of the Gatehouse on the western side. The most important of these was the north-side barn nearest the Court; having lost its roof in the hurricane, the cob was giving way and prior to its total collapse the timbers were salvaged by English Heritage. All that remains are Copeland's notes which state that this is 'a long barn built of cob, with a rectangular two-light transomed oak window; and there is another chamfered oak-framed opening to the south, besides an oak-framed doorway to the north, a door with fleurette hinges to the north-east, an oak-framed upper opening, an oak-framed triple-light iron-barred transomed rectangular window and a rectangular oak-framed triple-light window.'[10] Although not dated by Copeland, there was, according to a former farm employee, an engraved stone on the east wall of the barn with the date 1756.[11] This date would indicate that the work was undertaken by William Sanford, who had succeeded his father William Sanford as an infant in 1718. The date 1756 would accord with both Copeland's description of the north-side barn and with the surviving features of the west-side barn and the Gatehouse. Although most of these barns were accessed from the outer courtyard, those on the northern side were part of a second much smaller stable yard. Still in use in the 1950s, now only the ruined cob walls remain of this early 18th C stable block and shippon, which estate records show were built by Anne Sanford between 1720 and 1730.

Historically, Ayshford Court has been approached from two directions. The principal upper road from Westleigh still exists as a farm track on the northern side of the Court. This would have been the preferred route in winter, as the lower road crossed the flood plain and would often have been impassable. Benjamin Donn's map of 1765 (Frontispiece) shows that this lower road through Ayshford led down to a ford that crossed the River Lyner at Pugham and from there through Hounds Aller Farm to join the Tiverton-Wellington high road at a junction now known as Waterloo Cross. This southern approach to the Court had to be diverted when the canal was built, but its old line can still be seen leading up to the canal from the Westleigh road at the eastern end of the hamlet – plot 1001 on the Tithe map. From this point the road led directly into the south-east corner of the outer courtyard, passing over a culvert or channel connecting the two grist mill holding ponds, through the Gatehouse to the front of the Court. Since 1812, access from Ayshford to the Court has been from a slip road off the lower Westleigh Road opposite Ayshford House. This public road, which crosses the Grand Western Canal via a metal (formerly wood) accommodation bridge on stone abutments, now ends at Ayshford Court Farm. When first built by the Canal Company, this road is shown by Greenwood's survey of 1827 to have rejoined the old road from the village to the mill and chapel yard at the bottom of Brimstone Lane, thereby maintaining access from Ayshford Street to Holcombe Rogus, Whitnage and Sampford Peverell; the lane is now disused and has become totally overgrown.

Beside the modern farm buildings a stone pillar marks the start of a short private drive that skirts the north side of the house and garden and leads into the former inner courtyard. Since the late 1960s, when the land and farm buildings were sold off, this has become the only road entrance to the Court, although farm vehicles continue to use the track that passes through the old stable yard to the upper Westleigh road. Continuing on this track, halfway up the hill on the right-hand side and opposite the overgrown ruins of a house occupied by the dairyman until the 1960s, is a curving wall that provides a line for an old road, which could at one time have led to an entrance through the eastern side of the outer courtyard. However, the evidence of the 1841 tithe map and a plan attached to a conveyance, written in 1811 relating to the Grand Western Canal Company's purchase of Ayshford Sanford land along the route of the canal[12], together with the established position of the mid 18th C barns, shows that entrance to the Court had almost certainly always been made through the north-east and south-east corners of the outer courtyard.

---

[1] Enclosure to letter to Mrs Merry of Ayshford Court dated 10th April 10th 1964

[2] Polwhele, Rev. R. *The History of Devonshire* (3 vols) London 1793-1806 Vol 2 pp 367-8

[3] Cherry. B. and Pevsner, *The Buildings of England, Devon*. Ed.2. Penguin 1989 p.65

[4] A convex moulding of which the section is a quarter circle or quarter ellipse. *OED* Ed.3.1959

[5] Radford, CAR. 'Ayshford Court, Burlescombe'; *Devon & Cornwall Notes & Queries* 27 (1956-58) pp 196-8.

[6] To furnish with a canopy....to line the roof with woodwork to construct an inner roof. *OED* Ed.3.1959. This mediaeval term to 'ceil' particularly applies to the practice of inserting a ceiling in a great hall, thereby creating a private family room above it.

[7] Ibid, Radford, CAR.

[8] Enclosure to letter to Mrs Merry of Ayshford Court dated 10th April 1964

[9] The figure in the centre is so worn as to be indecipherable.

[10] Ibid.

[11] This may be the date of restoration of an ancient cob barn rather than replacement as the timbers that were rescued by English Heritage prior to its total collapse in the late 1990s were dendrologically assessed as mediaeval.

[12] For further details see the Ayshford Community and Fig.42

Figure 29. St Michael's Chapel from the south-west (Neil MacDonald)

AYSHFORD CHAPEL

The earliest surviving written record of a chapel at Ayshford is to be found in the cartulary [register] of Canonsleigh Priory dated 19 October 1282. This records the memorandum of an agreement by John Ayshford, Lord of Ayshford, and the villeins of the place, all of them parishioners of the church of Burlescombe, with the canons. In return for a quarterly payment of one shilling and six pence (£25) the canons were bound to celebrate mass in the chapel on Fridays and Sundays and the feasts of Christmas and Michaelmas. They were also required to baptise the lawful sons of the Lords of Ayshford and to church their wives. Although the Prior and his canons were forced to leave Canonsleigh when it became a convent in 1284, it would appear that this agreement was transferred to the Abbess and her appointed priest. In 1287 a libel action (subsequently withdrawn) relating to the chapel of Saint Michael of Ayshford was scheduled to be heard by an official of Bishop Peter Quinel of Exeter between John Ayshford, Lord of Ayshford, and his men, and the 'relygeus ladys abbas and convent' of Canonsleigh. This agreement was clarified in 1324 when Bishop Walter de Stapledon of Exeter 'ordained that since the Abbess and convent were bound to provide divine service on certain days of the year by their own priest in the chapel of Ayshford, the priest who celebrated there on Easter Day should, himself or through another priest of the abbey, administer the sacrament of the Eucharist to the parishioners of the church of Burlescombe, who by "accepted custom" were hearing services in the chapel.'[1]

By accepting the custom of administering the sacrament to all parishioners attending services in St. Michael's Chapel, Bishop Stapledon was authorising a practice that would continue for over six and half centuries, until the combination of parishes in the late 1980s forced the Rector to withdraw his regular monthly service. In 1383, as part of the evidence for William Ayshford as a ward of Royal Courts achieving the age of twenty-one, a number of witnesses certified that in 1362 the chapel had been used by parishioners for marriage services and baptisms. By 1434 it would seem that the priest appointed to administer to the Abbess and nuns at Canonsleigh was also Vicar of Burlescombe, for, according to Fursdon, it was the churchwardens who made the necessary application to Jonathon (sic) Bishop of Exeter for 'John Spiring Vicar to have a licence to serve in Ayshforde Chapple.'[2] Whether parish or convent was now responsible is unclear, but parochial duties were certainly maintained at the chapel until the Dissolution of the Monasteries in 1538, by which time the priest was paid £5 6s. 8d (£2000); a level of stipend that indicates he was probably acting as chaplain to the Ayshford community. This seems to be confirmed by Henry VIII's Survey of Chantries in 1546, which classified the priest of St. Michael's Chapel at Ayshford as 'stipendiary', thereby avoiding inevitable closure and probable destruction as a chantry.[3] The Ayshford family may well have taken on the responsibility for paying the priest's stipend from about this time and most of the subsequent Ayshford family wills include provision for the chaplain and maintenance of their chapel.

Although the present Grade I listed building (Fig.29) is almost certainly on the site of this original chapel, the lack of documentary evidence and extensive restoration and rebuilding over the past 500 years has made positive attribution questionable, if not impossible. Described by Risdon in 1609[4] as an 'ancient chapel' it seems to be generally accepted as mediaeval, probably around the turn of the 14-15th centuries, but a report to the Somerset Archaeological Society in 1912[5] gave evidence of much earlier stonework that had been used in its construction. Unlike the manorial buildings with which such domestic chapels or chapels-of-ease were associated, it would have been stone built with a walled chapel-yard that often included a wooden lean-to 'cell' for the priest. Confirmation of a 'spacious [chapel] yard contiguous to Ayshford Court' is provided by both Risdon and the Sanford archive, the yard being used for storage of timber in 1734[6], but the change in the landscape for construction of the canal in 1812 has removed any remaining evidence of this feature. Having lost the road to the chapel from both manor and village at the same time the only access now is on foot through a small iron gate near the pillared entrance to the Court. Crossing the field beside the canal, the visitor enters the chapel through the south door; the west door, the former main entrance, is now kept bolted.

Built of Westleigh chert stone with Beerstone details and diagonal volcanic stone buttresses under a Delabole slate roof, with a continuous Hamstone ridge, Ayshford Chapel is larger than most domestic chapels. The gable ends have shaped kneelers and coping, surmounted by a small apex cross at the east end and a small open-sided and gabled bell-cote at the west end. Having internal measurements of 11m x 4.4m (36ft x 14.5ft.) this small rectangular building is a church in miniature. There is sufficient room in the nave for 11 rough pews for three or four people, and

Figure 30. 15th century Chancel screen and wagon roof   *(Apex Photo Agency)*

two further pews in the chancel. The nave is separated from the chancel by a screen (Fig.30) beneath a heavy 15th C wagon roof with moulded purlins and carved oak bosses. There are three heavily restored two-light perpendicular style windows with plain hoodmoulds on both the north and south sides, and similar three-light windows above the altar in the chancel and over the west door. Although the studded oak doors with their massive strap-hinges are 19th C replacements, both doorways are probably original having two-centred archways and a moulded surround (Fig.31). Copeland noted that the 'moulds of the south doorway are particularly good ogee and roll with a more obtuse head than the west.' Some historians consider this doorway provides evidence of late Norman stonework that could have come from the original Ayshford Chapel or been taken from the ruins of another mediaeval chapel that was known to have existed at Canonsleigh.

Figure 31. South door (Apex Photo Agency)

The west doorway has 'soffit-shafts with bellneck caps and moulded octagonal bases on a square plinth.' The 15th C screen, which was one of the primary factors in the Grade 1 listing, was re-decorated in the mid-19th C with pastel shades of pink and blue and gilded. It has twelve bays with trifoliated heads and sunken spandrils and a central cusped four-centred doorway with 'carved spandrils to the soffit which spring from embattled corbels. There is a cornice of fleurone (or square "flowers") below an embattled mould or cresting.'[7]

If the earliest date is accepted, the most likely member of the Ayshford family to have paid for a new chapel was William Ayshford, whose marriage to Emma Ferrars in 1396 would have provided both the means to pay for it and the need to demonstrate his enhanced position in Devon society. The presence of so many 15th C features makes it less likely that Nicholas Ayshford (ca.1485-1557), as suggested by Radford, undertook the initial construction although he almost certainly carried out repairs and improvements. There is no evidence that the chapel was used for anything other than routine services, baptisms, marriages and churching until the 17th C. All burials took place at the Parish Church of St. Mary the Virgin at Burlescombe where Nicholas Ayshford had built the north (Ayshford) aisle and where his tomb can be seen in the sanctuary. The earliest of the three tombs in the Ayshford Chapel is that of Henry Ayshford (1576-1650) and his wife Amy, who are commemorated by a slab in front of the altar. The inscription is so worn

Figure 32. Henry Ayshford (1664-1666): sarcophagus tomb in the Chapel Sanctuary (Apex Photo Agency)

Figure 33. John Ayshford (ca.1641-1690) and his wife Susanna, daughter of Lucius Knightly: monument on the north wall of Ayshford Chapel nave (Neil MacDonald)

that it is now almost unreadable, but historians have the benefit of a detailed description of the chapel in 1828, by the then Rector of Burlescombe the Reverend Thomas Tanner[8] that provides information that would otherwise have been lost. 'The floor stone with armorial Bearings at the lower is a plain free stone within the communion rails – To Henry Ayshford Esq. he died in 1649 aged 73 – and to Amie his wife – she died 31 Oct. 1659 these inscriptions are in Latin.' Heather Ayshford's researches located an interesting letter relating to Henry Ayshford's funeral in the Trevelyan papers from John Ayshford, the younger son and excecutor, to John Willoughby of Payhembury. Having mentioned the death of his father and invited him to the funeral which was to be held 'in his own chapel' he adds in a post-script 'pray sir keep the day private', which she considered 'probably reflected his father's desire for a High (Laudian) Church service in a time of puritan zeal! Perhaps this was the last time that the waft of incense was to be detected in the chapel.'[9]

In the north-east corner of the sanctuary beside the altar is a sarcophagus tomb (Fig.32) with 'arms engraved 3 ashkeys between 2 chevrons date 1666 for Henry Ayshford aged 1 year 9 months departed this life the 17th day of January 1666 son of Arthur A: Esq.' The third memorial is a highly decorated wall monument now placed on the north wall (Fig.33), but in 1828 apparently situated in the south corner near the communion table 'the mural, very gaudy, similar to those in Burlescombe Church... richly ornamented with armorial bearings, cherubs, etc, to John Ayshford Esq. he dies Feb 24th 1689 [1690 by today's calendar] aged 49. I believe he

Figure 34. 19th century perpendicular style two and three-light mullioned stone windows
(Apex Photo Agency)

was the last of the line - & Susanna his wife daughter of Lucy (a singular name for a man) Knightley of London, Merchant – She died Dec. 6th 1668 aged 24. John Ayshford above bequeathed the sum of £15 per annum for the maintenance of Chapel for ever out of the Barton Estate'. [10]

Additionally, Tanner noted that 'within the memory of man' the chapel had a wooden cupola with five bells but only one remained after the bell-cote was rebuilt at some time around the turn of the 18-19th C. This bell, which is presently installed in the bell-cote, has the inscription *'This Bell is Henry Ayshford's. T.P. 1657.* [11] In 1828 the chapel sanctuary had a 'plain oak table within strong oak rails and a modern pulpit of Wainscott oak' but none of these items have survived. Similarly, the location of a large font, which had been recovered from the farmyard and reinstated in the chapel some twenty years previously, is unknown. Perhaps, like some of the glass from the chapel windows, this 'Ayshford family' heirloom was moved to another Sanford property. The Ayshford Chapel communion plate had clearly been 'lost' for many generations except for a flagon, engraved with the Ayshford arms, which was being used in Burlescombe Church.

Tanner's description of Ayshford Chapel in 1828 makes no mention of its overall condition but by 1847 Davidson records that 'Ayshford Chapel is now in course of repair and restoration at the cost of Ayshford Sanford esq. [Edward]. The new stone

Figure 35. Chapel chancel - central window of five with the words of the Te Deum in stained glass (Apex Photo Agency)

Figure 37. West end window - early 19th century (Neil MacDonald)

Figure 36. Detail - logo of stained glass artist John Toms of Wellington, Somerset
(Neil MacDonald)

windows are in perpendicular style formed by two and three lights with cinquefoil heads (Fig.34). The font is an ancient large circular stone basin without ornament. The monuments are removed for a time.' Three years later Davidson noted that repairs were still in hand being 'left till now in an unfinished state without doors and floor and the new windows without glass ... The ancient font lies neglected on the ground amidst unfinished stonework. Cattle and sheep take shelter in the building.'[12]

Repairs were completed by 1857 when Billings Directory[13] reported that the chapel 'had lately been restored with great taste' that included touching up the old screen and introducing new windows in the nave and chancel inscribed with the words of the Te Deum (Fig.35). These five windows and the two remaining matching windows at the west end of the nave were originally thought to be the work of Thomas Willement, but research undertaken by Jeanne James has confirmed that they were made by a local stained glass artist John Toms (1813-1867) from Wellington in Somerset, whose monogram can be seen in the bottom corner of each window (Fig.36). The origins of the earlier west-end window are unknown. It is almost certainly contemporary with the installation of the bell-cote at the turn of the 18-19th centuries and was presumably the only glazing that did not need to be replaced by Toms during the restoration of the chapel in the 1850s (Fig.37). Externally, the building was re-pointed and the 15th C 'putlog holes'[14] were filled with decorative stonework. Although some of these perforated quatrefoils survived, most became very weather-worn; they were replaced in the restoration of 2000-03 (Fig.38).

Figure 38. Putlog hole - restored 2003
(Apex Photo Agency)

Following Edward Ayshford Sanford's mid 19th C restoration, it seems from all the records that routine services were resumed by the Rectors of Burlescombe and continued by the Sampford Peverell Team Rectors when the livings were amalgamated in 1976. The last routine monthly service was held by the Reverend Michael Boyes in 1989. After the 1939-45 War little if anything was done to maintain the chapel and in the eleven years following the withdrawal of regular services, being unused and with only the occasional visitor to open the doors, the building steadily deteriorated. By 2000 it was in need of a second major restoration that was beyond the resources of the Ayshford Sanford family and it passed into the care of the Friends of Friendless Churches. The repairs, which were underwritten by a 70% grant from English Heritage, were undertaken by Arnold & Lang of Cullompton, supervised by the Friends' architect Louise Bainbridge of Seymour Bainbridge of Winchester, and completed in 2003.[15] (Fig.39)

---

[1] James, Jeanne, *Devon and Cornwall Notes and Queries* Vol 39 Part V pp.129-130; Reprinted for Friends of Friendless Churches in the *Transactions of the Ancient Monuments Society*. London, V.C.M. ed. *The Cartulary of Canonsleigh Abbey* Harleian MS No.3660.

[2] Fursdon, C.A.T. *Collection of Church Notes – Devon Parishes Church Rates* 1926-27 Typescript West Country Studies Library. The submission to Jonathon is at odds with Cathedral historical records as Edmund Lacey was Bishop of Exeter at this time

[3] For further information see Orme, Prof. N. 'Dissolution of the Chantries in Devon, 1546-8' *Report and Transactions of the Devonshire Association 111* (1979) pp 75-123

[4] Polwhele, R. *The History of Devonshire* (3 Vols) London 1793-1806 Vol.2. p.369; Risdon.T. *The Geographical Description or Survey of the County of Devon*, London 1811.

[5] Bond, B. Ayshford Chapel and Manor House, *Somersetshire Archaeological and Natural History Society Proceedings lviii* (1912) pp.47-48.

[6] Somerset Record Office, Sanford Estate documents, *DD/SF/3/3/15*

[7] Enclosure to letter to Mrs Merry of Ayshford Court dated 10th April 1964

[8] Davidson, J.B. transcription. *Notes on Devon Churches – East Devon* West Country Studies Library microfiche p.569-71

[9] Somerset Record Office *DD/WO 57/13/5*. Heather Ayshford's comments taken from personal correspondence with the author.

[10] Davidson, J.B. ibid. p.571. Both the 1744 and 1779 Diocesan Visitation Returns for Burlescombe, published by the Friends of the Devon Archives, include in the report on Chapels in the Parish that this annual stipend of £15 continued to be paid to the Minister by 'Ye Sanfords of Nynehead Court, Somerset, heirs of Ayshford'.

[11] Research by Jeanne James records that this stands for Thomas Petherington, an Exeter Bell Founder.

[12] Davidson, J.B. ibid. p.572. This is the last reference to the font.

[13] Billing, M. *Directory and Gazetteer of the County of Devon*, Birmingham 1857 (see Burlescombe p.220)

[14] Putlog Holes – 'apertures normally filled with stones that are sometimes un-mortared and have fallen out into which scaffolding poles were slotted when the building was under construction' (Jeanne James), attention to which was drawn by E Bligh Bond in Note 3 to his article 'Ayshford Chapel and Manor House', *Somersetshire Archaeological and Natural History Society Proceedings* 1912

[15] Further details of the 1847-55 and 2000-03 restorations are contained in the article by Jeanne James and Matthew Saunders in Volume 48 of the *Transactions of the Ancient Monuments Society*.

Figure 39. St Michael's Chapel undergoing repairs for Friends of Frendless Churches 2002 (Christopher Dalton)

THE AYSHFORD COMMUNITY
(Formerly known as Ayshford Street)

From Ayshford Bridge the visitor can easily see the full extent of the hamlet that once encompassed more than two dozen households and was known as Ayshford Street, but now, excluding the Court and its modern Home Farm bungalow, just consists of Ayshford House, a farm and four farm cottages (Fig.40). Stated by Polwhele at the turn of the 18-19th centuries as having 'one large street, in which live some serge-makers, but the trade is at present not very considerable'[1], the rapid decline in the rural population created by the industrial revolution destroyed communities like Ayshford, often leaving little evidence of their existence. Only three houses shown in the Tithe Survey of 1839 still exist: Ayshford Cottage [renamed Ayshford House in 1890], Bowdens [renamed Lower Ayshford Farm in the 1930s] and Lower Ayshford Dairy [now known by its 17th C name as Locks Cottage]. The foundations of some of the more substantial buildings can still be seen or have been converted into farm sheds, but most of those cottages, being built of cob with thatched roofs, have disappeared without trace.

Ayshford as a community has existed since Saxon times, providing the manor with its villeins and serfs, but like the houses they lived in, they left no evidence of their individual existence. Domesday records that the Ayshford manor was supported by '4 villans, 7 bordars and 3 serfs', suggesting that in Norman times the hamlet consisted of at least fourteen cottages. Its successor, conducted during the reigns of Henry III and Edward I, was Testa de Nevill, but this survey gives no figures for the population as it was only required to provide the names of those

Figure 40. Ayshford House, Lower Ayshford Farm and Ayshford cottages from the canal towpath (Neil MacDonald)

responsible for paying the Crown's fee[2]. The most complete mediaeval survey of the population was provided by a series of Lay Subsidies conducted between 1290 and 1334 [Edward I, Edward II and Edward III]; these were used to pay for Parliamentary expenses, such as Edward III's campaign against Scotland in 1327. Although some individuals and groups were excluded, as were those deemed to have possessions worth less than six shillings (£81.50), these returns provide a valuable insight into the distribution of wealth, and the location of an estimated two-thirds of the population. The most complete surviving record for Devon was for 1332[3], which included a separate listing for the manor of Ayshford in the Hundred of Halberton.[4] For this subsidy John de Ayshford (1290-ca.1336) was assessed for a payment of 18d (£21), and his ten manorial tenants[5] were required to provide a further 138d (£161). Unfortunately, these Lay Subsidies were the last surveys to identify individual manors within the parish of Burlescombe. All subsequent surveys, including the *Devon Subsidy Roll 1524-7, Subsidy Roll 1581, Protestation Return 1641-42 and Hearth Tax 1674* [6], provide lists of names that can only be placed within the parish by supporting evidence from other sources.

After a gap of nearly two centuries, from 1332 to the Subsidy Roll of 1525, it is hardly surprising that the only family name that can positively be identified is that of Nicholas Ayshford (1485-1557), though two households in the Burlescombe Parish list have the surname Trykhay that could well be descended from Thomas Trecchere. The Ayshford Sanford archive includes a large number of tenancy records, including one three-life lease[7], granted by Nicholas Ayshford (1507-1585) in September 1579 to John Rewe for Ayshford Meade, and another for the same property granted by his grandson, Henry Ayshford (1576-1650), in February 1619 to Thomas Markes a weaver[8], but it is not until 1662 that the population of the village can be confidently assessed. Following the death of Henry Ayshford (1640-1662), an Ayshford Manorial Roll was compiled with a full list of the 16 three-life tenants and their ages[9]; when the bailiff and other Ayshford Court domestic staff are taken into account, there must have been a minimum of twenty households, giving a total population, including children, of about eighty. Of particular interest is the extent to which this group of working men and women moved from place to place, for only John Webber and William Courton of the eligible men from this list of 1662 (aged at least 39) had signed the Burlescombe Protestation return in 1641. Martin Hellyar (alias Knowles), who had been granted the lease of a house in the village and 8.5 acres in April 1637, joined the Ayshford signatories in 1641, but gave up the tenancy and so was not included in the roll of 1662. Twelve years later, when the Hearth Tax of 1674 was compiled, seven of those sixteen tenancies had been retained; namely Edward Bowerman [Bowderman], Richard Bowdon [Bowden], Humphrey Garnsey, William Courtney [Courton], Jonathon Webber, George Alford and John Atkins (Pauper), with Thomas Courton, who had been given a copyhold labour tenement in May 1642[10]. It seems likely that the Webbers came to the village in the early part of the 17th C, when Nicholas Webber was appointed as Reeve for the Manor by Roger Ayshford[11]: the property with its surrounding meadows, which was at the lower end of the village, being known as Webbers until the late 18th C. The other property to retain the name of its builder was Bowdens. Humphrey Bowdon, clothworker, came to the village around 1650, receiving a lease from Henry Ayshford (1576-1650) for a messuage in the middle of the street; renewed by his son Richard in 1668, it remained in the Bowden family for 99 years until around 1750, when it was taken on by John Broom. The Bowden association was acknowledged by Fursdon: 'Bowden named after Richard Bowden or his father lived there in 1670. Paid rate of 3 pence and 1 penny for his close in 23rd year of reign of Charles II [By Act of Parliament Charles II's reign was deemed to have started in 1649 following the death of his father Charles I][12].

By the end of the 17th C Ayshford Street consisted of around a dozen properties, with leases granted between 1681 and 1704 to tenants with a wide variety of employment: Thomas Bowerman joiner, Richard Shepherd weaver, Richard Bowden clothworker, Charles Alford woolcomber, Richard Garnsey cordwainer, Richard Hellyar and Thomas Rowe smallholders. Their individual rentals varied from 2s 6d (£30) to over £9 (£1140), according to the amount of land they took on and whether they were committed to 7 or more days work on the estate[13]. Over the next 50 years the population of the village started to expand again. William Sanford (ca.1660-1718), and his son William (1717-1770), built five new cottages in the village, the first of which was leased to Elizabeth Evans in January 1705, three were taken on by Thomas Woolcott, woolcomber, in March 1716 and the last by John Evans in May 1727[14]. A water-powered grist mill with its holding ponds was built on the slope below the chapel at about the same time, and Francis Shallis, miller, was given a cottage and messuage in the village. In 1726 John Garnsey was given authority to convert one of the village barns to a tan-house, and to create a tan-yard on the adjacent plot for a peppercorn rent[15].

By 1750, when John Broom sergemaker took over the lease for Bowdens, Ayshford Street had already gained a reputation for work in the wool trade. In 1751, Broom obtained cover from Sun Fire Insurance to insure his 'workhouse, warehouse and stable under one roof, stone cob and thatched for £100; household goods and stock therein for £300', which had all been moved to 'Bowdens in Ayshford Street'. Three years later in 1754 his business had expanded, with an additional property called Blacklands 'all stone cob and thatched', requiring his cover to be increased to £600. The location of Blacklands was not stated in the policy, but was presumably in Kentisbeare, for in 1760 he took on a second house in the street [Ayshford] for his woolcomber and an 'additional' property in Kentisbeare, increasing his cover to £800[16].

Unfortunately, this period of relative prosperity was short-lived, for the introduction of industrial machinery in the new mills in Tiverton and Uffculme made home-weaving progressively less profitable. According to Polwhele, by the end of the 18th C the sergemaker's trade in Ayshford Street was in decline. Fifty years later, the 1841 and 1851 census returns show that it had disappeared completely. The village population, which had peaked at about a hundred in 1760 with over 20 families living in the 'street', declined to about a dozen houses and cottages (Fig.41). Agricultural labourers were still needed by the manor, and there were other trades that maintained a reasonable level of employment in the village; with the arrival of the 'navvies' in 1811, to build the Grand Western Canal, at least the Red Ball 'beerhouse' must have been a thriving establishment for a few years. The village lost two cottages in the path of the canal and the road to the Court was diverted, but otherwise the shape of the village was unaffected. The last of the holding ponds feeding the grist mill beside the chapel, was retained, allowing the mill to continue operating for another 50 years; in 1860 this pond was filled in and the mill replaced by a new water mill that formed part of the Court's outer courtyard.

Between 1810 and 1840 the number of occupied dwellings continued to fall, so, by 1841, the year of the first detailed census, there were 11 empty properties with only 25 adults and 12 children in the whole of the village, which included Ayshford Court's tenant farmer Nathaniel Cook, his wife Sarah, and their domestic and farm staff. Nathaniel Cook had become the tenant in 1834, when he was 26, taking over from John Hodges, with a rental payment of £449 (£3220)[17]. He would remain at the Court for the rest of his life; he died in 1878 when the lease was taken on by his son, William. From this low point in 1841 there was a rapid recovery; within ten years every house in the street was occupied, the population had more than doubled, reaching 86 in 1851, and Edward Ayshford Sanford was investing in new cottages for three of his tenants. The majority were still agricultural labourers, but three were described in the census return as 'gent' or of 'independent means', and there were three tradesmen, Simon Hitchcock, a cordwainer (boot- and shoe-

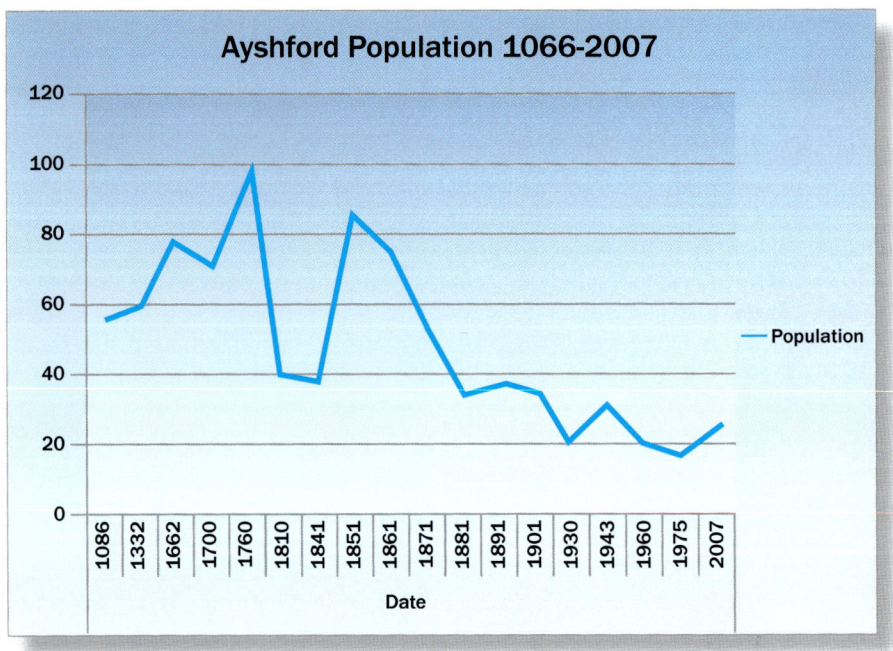

Figure 41. (Peter Bowers)

maker), Robert Hutchings, the estate miller, and Thomas Hurford, a lime brewer[18]. After 1861 the number of properties and the population slowly declined, so that all that remains of the original 'street' today are Ayshford House (Ayshford Cottage), Lower Ayshford Farm (Bowdens) and Locks Cottage (Lower Ayshford Dairy). All of the old cob and thatch cottages have disappeared, though some of their remains can still be identified. The population reached its lowest point at the end of the 19th C, the 1901 census recording just six inhabited properties in Ayshford, with 16 adults and children. There was little change over the succeeding seventy years, except for a temporary unrecorded spike between 1941 and 1945, when, it is understood, three or four families were billeted in Ayshford Court and Ayshford House. By 1975, with one new farm bungalow built, there were seven occupied dwellings and a total population of eighteen. Today, a further two properties brings the total to nine, providing accommodation for nineteen adults and six children.

The only published maps that provide any details of Ayshford's 'street', prior to publication in 1841 of the 1839 Tithe Commissioner's Survey, are the Grand Western Canal Company's survey by Robert Whitworth in 1769 (superimposed with the original canal route for submission to Parliament for the Navigation Act of 1796), a new Canal Company plan, produced in 1810 (superimposed with the amended route for the canal as part of their submission to Parliament for the Navigation Act of 1811), and a far less detailed Ordnance Surveyor's drawing published in 1801[19]. None of these three maps can be said to give more than a rough outline of the properties that made up the 'street'. However, a conveyance produced in 1811 for William Ayshford Sanford, listing all relevant properties in his Ayshford and Burlescombe estate that were to be acquired by the Canal Company, was accompanied by an estate map (Fig.42) with the exact route of the canal superimposed. It will be seen that this map, which has been annotated with the names of individual properties, shows Ayshford Court, the chapel and all cottages and buildings in the 'street'. As the plan of Ayshford Court includes all barns known to have been completed prior to 1750, but omits the mid-18th C addition of the rebuilt Gatehouse and southern side of the outer courtyard, and also shows the chapel with its 5-bell cupola, which was removed in the late 18th C, this map is most probably based on an estate survey produced around 1760, which no longer survives.

At the head of the village, between the track leading into the chapel yard and the old road to the Court, the Red Ball was a well-established ale-house, run on a part-time basis, or by an 'alewife', though the earliest record of a beer-houseman or innkeeper is in the 1841 Census, when Richard and Mary Hewett held the lease. The ale-house served a vital communal role in virtually every community, however small, and larger villages had several; Westleigh at this time had two, the White Ball and the Horse and Jockey, as well as a rather more up-market establishment, the Farmer's Hotel. The foundations of the Red Ball, which ceased trading in about 1860, together with its adjacent cottage, Broomfields, can still be seen in the grounds of Ayshford House, as can the remains of the cobbled road that once led past the front doors of these properties. It seems likely that Ayshford House (Fig.43)

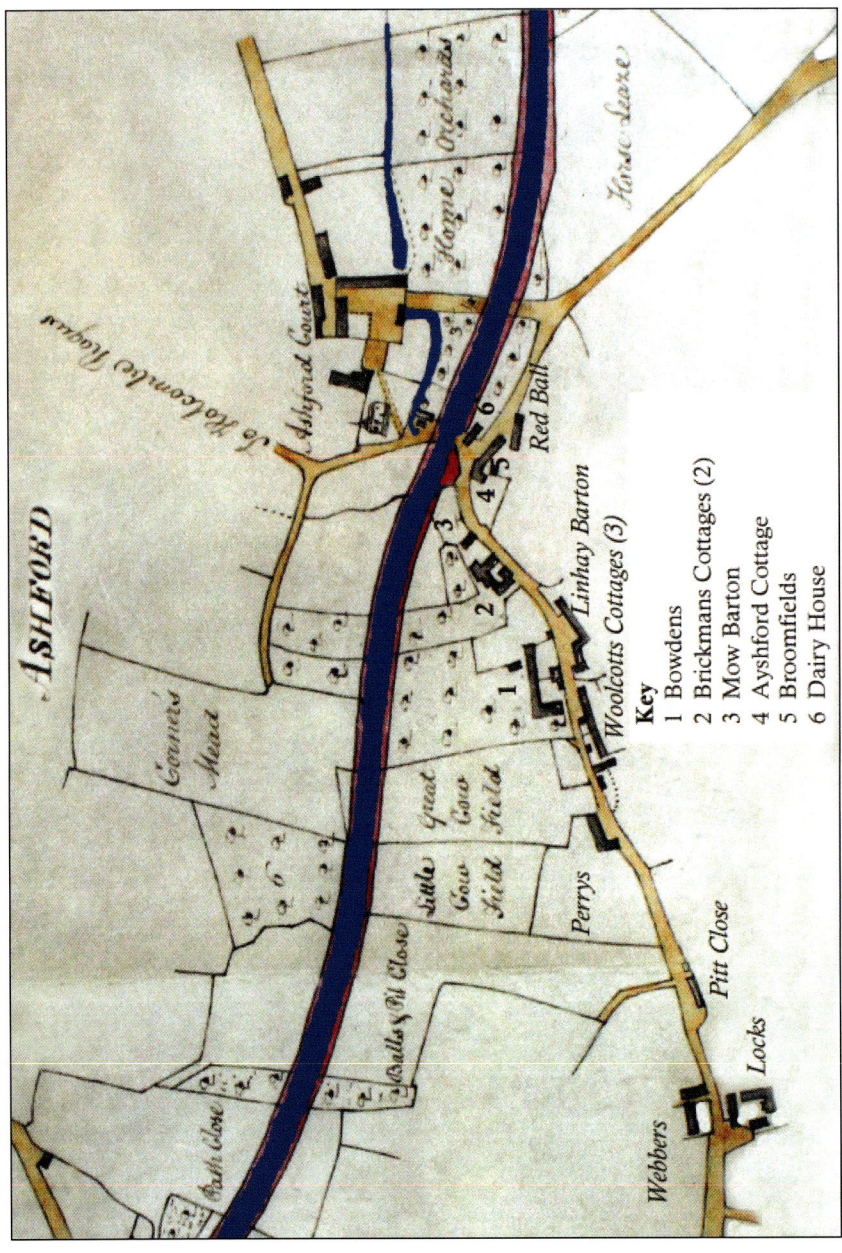

Figure 42. Ayshford estate map (ca. 1760), superimposed with the amended route of the Grand Western Canal, attached to the Ayshford Sanford conveyance of 1811 for the transfer of land and property to the Canal Company (Devon Record Office)

was built on the foundations of an older cottage, by William Sanford for his agent, around 1760, at the same time as major improvements were being undertaken to the Ayshford Court farm buildings. As the Court was then permanently occupied by farm tenants, Ayshford House was used to provide accommodation for a succession of Ayshford Sanford agents, and then for private tenants until sold, with the rest of the Ayshford Court farm estate, to Charles Home-Smith in 1938; he sold it on as a private property in 1939. Having a late Georgian appearance, successive owners had always considered the house to be early 19th C, but recent renovations exposed construction techniques that established the earlier date. Typically, costs had been kept to a minimum by using second-hand materials from adjacent redundant cottages, and pieces of Tudor and 17thC timbers were found to have been used by the builders. They also incorporated an adjacent 17th C cottage as an annexe, to serve as its kitchen, retaining the original fireplace and mantel and two pine doors. The house, which was known as Ayshford Cottage until about 1890, was extended into land bordering the new road in the 19th C, to provide modern sanitation and additional accommodation.

The two semi-detached stone and brick houses, on the opposite side of the road and immediately beneath the canal bridge, now known as Ayshford Cottages (Fig.44), were built by Edward Ayshford Sanford prior to 1860, probably as replacements for the Dairy House and Mow Barton cottages that were destroyed when the canal was built and two 'street' cottages, known as Brickman's[20] that used to exist in the

Figure 43. Ayshford House (formerly Ayshford Cottage) (ca. 1760), from the garden   *(Colin Findlay)*

Figure 44. Ayshford cottages (ca. 1860) from the south   (Neil MacDonald)

field below them. The original stone footbridge, which crossed the roadside stream and led to Mow Barton, was inadvertently destroyed by the District Council when undertaking flood prevention measures in the 1990s. Although much modified, Lower Ayshford Farm (Fig.45), formerly Bowdens, is the oldest surviving house in the 'street'. As previously mentioned, it was identified by Fursdon in 1670, as the property of Richard Bowden or his father, both of whom were living there in 1662: their absence from the Protestation list of 1641 implies that the land on which Bowdens was built was probably leased from Henry Ayshford (1640-1662) around the time of the Restoration. The lease of the property was originally made out for a tenement and about 4 acres of orchard and meadow (Bowden's Mead). It remained as a business premises until the mid 19th C, when Nathaniel Cook at Ayshford Court was farming 338 acres, mostly above the canal, and Will James of Sampford Peverell acquired Bowdens with around 70 acres below the canal. According to the 1851 and 1861 census returns, he never lived in the village, and the house was occupied by farm labourers. He appears to have given up his lease in the late 1860s, for, since 1871 Bowdens has been known as Lower Ayshford Farm, being run as a traditional dairy farm until the end of the 20th C. Little remains of Linhay Barton on the opposite side of the road except for two walls of a cattle shed that recently lost its roof and is scheduled to be replaced.

After Lower Ayshford Farm, with its engineering works and new bungalow, the road continues on its original track towards Holbrook, with nothing to show for the six cottages known as Woolcotts, Perrys, Pitt Close and Webbers, to Lock's Cottage (Fig.46). The origin of this name cannot be determined, as only one lease, to Thomas Rowe of Sampford Peverell in March 1687[21], refers to this tenement by that name. The 1839 Tithe Survey includes Lock's Orchard, but the farmhouse itself has been known as (Lower) Ayshford Dairy for generations, with tenant farmers working between 30 and 90 acres of pasture between the road and the River Lyner. Both Lock's Cottage and its dairy house, converted into a small cottage in 2001 and known as Swallows, almost certainly have much older origins or foundations, but there is now nothing visible that remains of interest. In the early 20th C, when John Merrey held the lease of Ayshford Court, and James Parr, dairyman, gave up his tenancy of Locks, the Ayshford Court farm estate was divided; 232 acres was retained by Ayshford Court and 168 acres was given to Lower Ayshford Farm. In 1939, John Merrey's son Frank Merrey, acquired Ayshford Court and its home farm from Charles Home-Smith. Some thirty years later, the Court and its home farm were separated, and in 1978 the remainder of the Ayshford Barton estate, Lower Ayshford Farm and Lock's cottage, was sold by Home-Smith to his sitting tenants.

With both Ayshford Court and Lower Ayshford farms having new agricultural tied houses, and the dairy house conversion at Locks Cottage, there are now nine families living in the village, and its population has been somewhat restored. However, with 19 adults and only six children of school age, the balance between old and young in 2008 is markedly different from earlier times. Further expansion is highly unlikely, as Ayshford is not a community earmarked for development by the District Council, unless the old Court barns can be converted. Nevertheless, this small community, which has retained its identity for well over a thousand years, seems set to continue for many generations to come. In time, those magnificent oaks that frame the visitor's view of this historic Court and its chapel from the canal, will be lost, but the buildings and the families, who live in this ancient community, seem certain to remain.

Figure 45. Lower Ayshford Farm (formerly Bowdens) ca. 1660 (Neil MacDonald)

Figure 46. Locks Cottage (formerly Lower Ayshford Dairy) (19th century on earlier foundations)
(Neil MacDonald)

---

[1] Polwhele, Richard. *The History of Devonshire (3 vols)*, London 1793-1806. Vol.2 p.367

[2] Testa de Nevill lists the name of Agnes Ayshford for Ayshford and William de Clavill for Burlescombe and Boehill. Devon section transcribed in *Transactions of the Devonshire Association Vol.30*. 1898 pp.203-37 stated to relate to the end of the reign of Edward I (1272-1307).

[3] The Lay Subsidy of 1332 transcribed in *Transactions of the Devon and Cornwall Record Society (New Series) Vol 14*. Ed.Erskine, A. Devonshire Press 1969

[4] Although Ayshford is in Burlescombe Parish it is properly placed in the Halberton Hundred, but for most returns it is included with Burlescombe in the Bampton Hundred.

[5] The Ayshford tenants were Walter Colman, Thomas Treccere, Simon Breghe, Thomas le Heir, Adam atte Wille, Thomas le Hurt, Roger atte More, Stephen Maister, Laurence Hore and John Hake. The majority were assessed for a minimum payment of 8d (£9) indicating 'villein' or 'bordar' status but Thomas le Hurt assessed for 2s 4d (£61), Roger atte More for 2s (£56) and Thomas Treccere for 20d (£23) were tradesmen living in the village whose stock was taken into account.

[6] Stoate, T.L. ed. *Devon Lay Subsidy Rolls 1524-7*. Devon Books 1979; Stoate, T.L. ed *Devon Taxes 1581-1660*. Devon Books 1988; Howard,A.J.ed *Devon Protestation Returns 1641*. Devon Books 1973; Stoate,T.L.ed. *Devon Hearth Tax Return, Lady Day 1674*. Devon Books 1982

[7] Mediaeval tenancies were tied to three names. In addition to his own the prospective tenant would choose two persons who could continue the tenancy after his death. These would usually be his wife and eldest son or daughter. During the life of any of these three the lease could be renewed by the payment of 'heriot' for a maximum of 99 years. On the death of the last life, unless heriot had been paid for three new lives, the tenancy would immediately revert to the landlord, irrespective of who was living there or for how long, and the occupants would be thrown out on the street.

[8] Somerset Record Office Sanford Estate documents *DD/SF/2/70/7 and 70/14*

[9] James Bowdman (60), James Bowdman jun (30); George Alford (45) & widow; Elizabeth Shopway (67), John Shopway (70); John Webber (80) & wife (69), Edward Webber (35); William Courton (42), brother John Courton (40); John Courton (58), Joanna Courton (54), James Courton (38); Richard Bowden (35), Mary Bowden; Margaret Garraby (64), Mary Haynes (25); Humphrey Garnsey (40), Mary Garnsey (45); Johanna Webber (75) & daughter (45); William Holby (47); Edward Bowderman (40), Martin Bowderman (38), Emmanuel Bowderman (15); Thomas Courton & widow by Heriot to Richard (18), Mary (20) & Abigale (18); John Atkins (48), Mary Atkins (22); Robert Turner (53); Jeffrey Edwards (62), John Edwards (30).

[10] Stoate,T.L.ed. *Devon Hearth Tax Return, Lad y Day 1674*. Devon Books 1982 - Burlescombe Parish

[11] Nicholas Webber submitted the Ayshford Manor accounts as Reeve in 1610.

[12] Fursdon, C.A.T. *Collection of Church Notes – Devon Parishes Church Rates 1926-27* Typescript West Country Studies Library

[13] Somerset Record Office Sanford Estate documents *DD/SF/2/70/8,70/9,70,51,70/63*

[14] Somerset Record Office Sanford Estate documents *DD/SF/2/70/66*

[15] Somerset Record Office Sanford Estate documents *DD/SF/2/70/71*

[16] Sun Fire Insurance Co. Records 1726-1770. Included in Sanford MS Somerset Record Office. A field known as Blacklands is shown on the 1839 Tithe map below the Sampford Peverell-Westleigh road but no dwelling existed at that time.

[17] Somerset Record Office Sanford Estate documents *DD/SF/2/70/86*

[18] Ancestry.co.uk – Devon 1841-1901 Census Returns – Burlescombe Parish.

[19] Copies of the Grand Western Canal Company's original and amended routes of the canal and the Ordnance Survey's Surveyors' 3 inch drawings 1801 sheet 41 Part 1 together with the 1839 Tithe Commissioners' Survey published 1841 and the Conveyance of Ayshford Sanford land in Devon to the Canal Company (Quarter Sessions, Vol. 1. Guide 44, Canal Companies' enrolled deeds. Ref: 44/2 WA Sanford), are held by the Devon Record Office.

[20] Part of a wall from the Dairy House can be seen in the canal bank near the gate in the small field opposite Ayshford House but nothing remains of Mow Barton or Brickman's cottages.

[21] Somerset Record Office Sanford Estate documents *DD/SF/2/70/32*

BIBLIOGRAPHY AND OFFICIAL RECORDS

Bibliography

Ayshford, F. and H. Notes towards a history of the Ayshford family of Devon, Private publication 2007

Barlow, F. Intro. The Devonshire Domesday, Alecto Historical Editions 1991

Billing, M. Directory and Gazetteer of the County of Devon, Birmingham 1857 et.seq.

Bond, B. Ayshford Chapel and Manor House, Somersetshire Archaeological and Natural History Society Proceedings 1912

Cherry, B. and Pevsner, N. The Buildings of England, 2nd Edition. Penguin 1989

Copeland, G.W. Private letter to Mrs Peter Merrey of Ayshford Court, April 1964

Davidson, J.B. Notes on Devon Churches – East Devon, West Country Studies Library

Fursdon, C.A.T. Collection of Church Notes – Devon Parishes Church Rates 1926-27. Typescript West Country Studies Library

Gover, J.E.B. Mawer, A. & Stenton, F.M. The Place Names of Devon, CUP 1932

Harris, H. The Grand Western Canal, David & Charles 1973

Hooke, D. Pre-Conquest Charter Bounds of Devon and Cornwall, Woodbridge 1994

Howard, A.J. ed. Devon Protestation Returns 1641, Devon Books 1973

James, J. and Saunders, M. The Friends of Friendless Churches: Chapel of St. Michael, Ayshford, Burlescombe, Devon, Transactions of the Ancient Monuments Society 2004

Lysons, D. and S. Magna Britannia vi, Topographical and Historical Account of Devonshire (2 vols), London 1822

Nynehead & District Local History Society. The History of Nynehead, Halsgrove 2003

Officer, L.H. and Williamson, S.H. www.measuringworth.com, financial calculator

Orme, Prof. N. Dissolution of the Chantries in Devon, 1546-8, Transactions of the Devonshire Association 1979

Polwhele, Rev.R. The History of Devonshire (3 vols), London 1793-1806

Radford, C.A.R. Ayshford Court, Burlescombe, Devon & Cornwall Notes & Queries 1956

Risdon, T. The Geographical Description or Survey of the County of Devon, London 1811

Scott-Fox, C. Ed. Sampford Peverell, The Village, Church, Chapel and Rectories, Sampford Peverell Society 2005

Stoate, T.L. ed. Devon Hearth Tax Return, Lady Day 1674, Devon Books 1982

Stoate, T.L. ed. Devon Lay Subsidy Rolls 1524-7, Devon Books 1979

Stoate, T.L. ed. Devon Taxes 1581-1660, Devon Books 1988

Uffculme Archive Group. Uffculme, a Peculiar Parish. 1997

Worth, R.N. A History of Devonshire, Elliot Stock, London 1886

Official Records

Devon Record Office - card indexes, Ayshford and Burlescombe Parish and Grand Western Canal records

Ordnance Survey – 1801 Surveyor's 3 inch drawings

Oxford Shorter English Dictionary – 3rd Edition 1959

Proceedings of the Somersetshire Archaeological and Natural History Society

Somerset Record Office - Sanford Estate documents DD/SF series

Transactions of the Ancient Monuments Society

Transactions of the Devon and Cornwall Record Society

Transactions of the Devonshire Association

West Country Studies Library – Devon County publications and Burnett-Morris Index

Appendix 1

THE AYSHFORD INHERITANCE AND FAMILY TREE
1086 - 1485

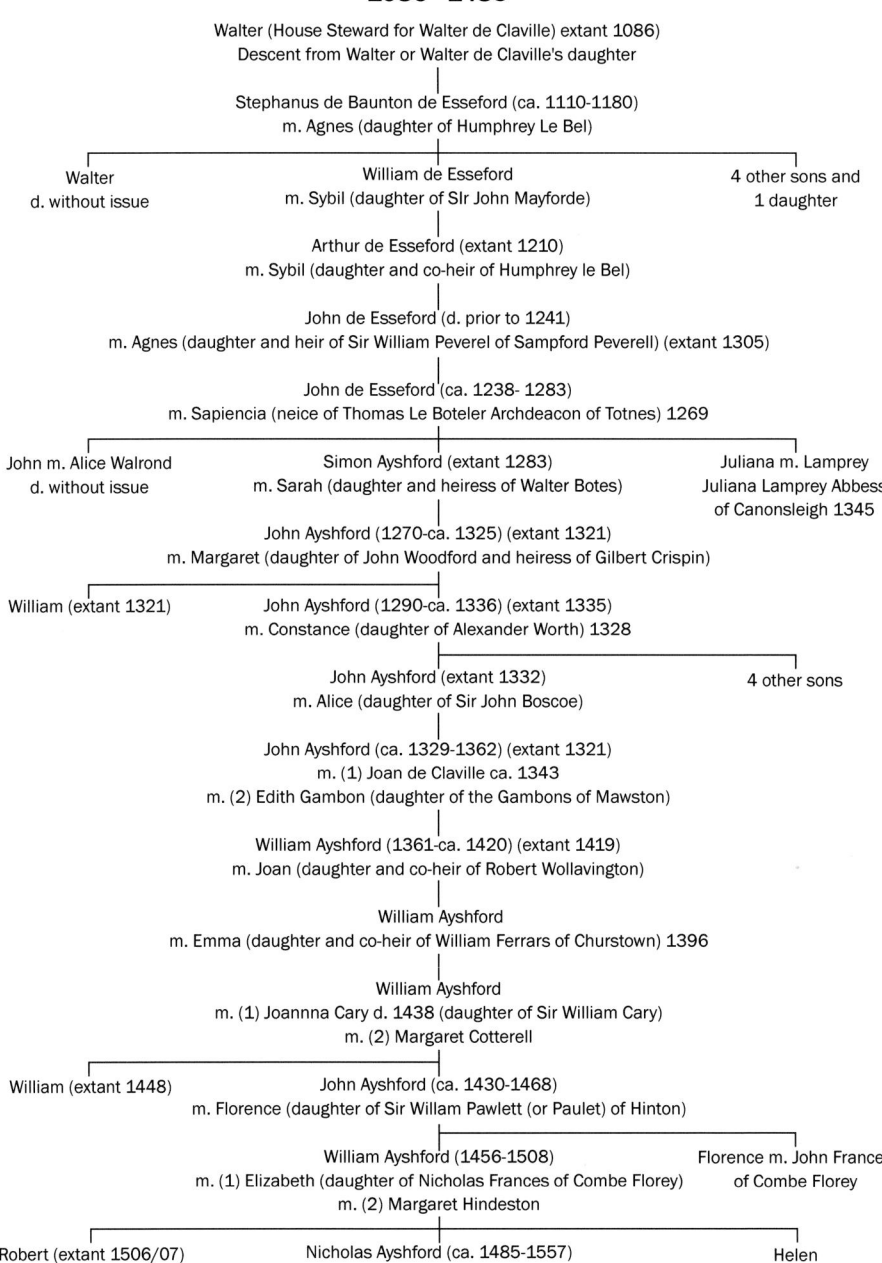

THE AYSHFORD INHERITANCE AND FAMILY TREE
1485 - 1701

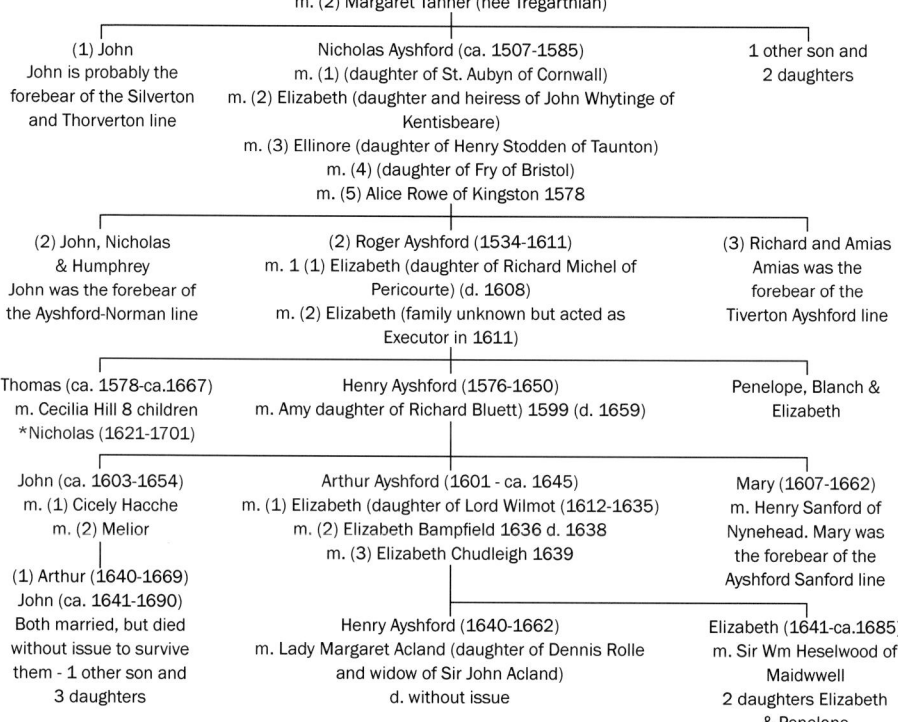

Estate entailed to the descendants of Henry Ayshford (1576-1650)
On the death of his grandson Henry Ayshford (1640-1662) the estate passed successively to
1662 - His cousin Arthur Ayshford whose heir and only son Henry died 1666
1669 - Arthur's brother JHn Ayshfrod whose wife Susanna Knightly died 1668 without issue
1690 - His late Aunt Mary's second son John Sanford MP
(See Appendix 2)

*Nicholas Ayshford (1621-1701), who was the last surviving male descendant of Roger Ayshford, was the residue beneficiary of John Ayshford's estate after John Sanford MP. In 1700 he sold his interest in the estate to John Sanford for £3000 (£360,000) using most of the proceeds to found Uffculme Grammar School

Appendix 2

THE SANFORD INHERITANCE AND FAMILY TREE

John Sanford, Lord of Brook Sanford (-1380)

Martin Sanford (-1643)
m. Susan Sydenham. Purchased Nynehead ca. 1599

Henry Sanford (1612-1644)
m. Mary Ayshford (sister of Henry Ayshford and heiress of John Ayshford)

John Sanford MP Taunton & Minehead 1688-95 (1638-1711)
m. Elizabeth Knightly

William Sanford (ca.1660-1718)
m. Anne Clarke

William Sanford (1717-1770)
m. Anne Chichester

John Sanford (ca.1740-1779)
m. Hon. Jane Anstruther

William Ayshford Sanford (1772-1833)
m. Mary Marshall

Edward Ayshford Sanford MP Taunton 1830-41 (1794-1872)
m. (1) Henrietta Langham
m. (2) Lady Caroline Stanhope

William Ayshford Sanford (1818-1902)
m. (1) Ellen Seymour
m. (2) Sarah Hervey

Colonel Edward Ayshford Sanford of Chipley (1857-1923)
m. May Griffiths

William Ayshford Sanford (1905-1974)
m. Rosemary Lindsay

Edward William Ayshford Sanford (b. 1929)
m. Judy Vickery

Edward Samuel Ayshford Sanford (b. 1978)